UNDER FIRE IN THE DARDANELLES

UNDER FIRE IN THE DARDANELLES

The Great War Diaries & Photographs
of MAJOR EDWARD CADOGAN

Foreword by
Viscount Chelsea

Edited by
Kira Charatan and Camilla Cecil

Pen & Sword
MILITARY

First published in Great Britain by
PEN & SWORD MILITARY
an imprint of
Pen & Sword Books Limited
47 Church Street, Barnsley
S. Yorkshire, S70 2AS

ISBN 1 84415 374 6

A CIP catalogue record for this book
is available from the British Library.

Designed and typeset in 10pt Sabon
by Sylvia Menzies, Pen & Sword Books Ltd

Printed and bound in Great Britain by
CPI UK

Pen & Sword Books Ltd incorporates the imprints of
Pen & Sword Aviation, Pen & Sword Maritime, Pen & Sword Military,
Pen & Sword Select, Pen & Sword Military Classics,
Leo Cooper and Wharncliffe Local History.

For a complete list of Pen & Sword titles please contact:
PEN & SWORD BOOKS LIMITED
47 Church Street, Barnsley, South Yorkshire, S70 2AS, England.
E-mail: enquiries@pen-and-sword.co.uk
Website: www.pen-and-sword.co.uk

Contents

Foreword by
Viscount Chelsea

❦

The diaries in this book came to light in the year 2000. My grandfather (the 7th Earl Cadogan) had recently died and so my family and I were busy moving into Snaigow, the family home in Perthshire. We were about to begin renovation work on the estate, so we were packing up anything and everything. One day, our handyman who was helping with this – Ted Downham – asked the question that now leads me to write this foreword. 'There are all these crates in one of the barns', he said. 'What do you want doing with them during the renovations?'

I was surprised; no-one had ever mentioned them to me before. I went up into the loft of the barn to see just what sort of rubbish this might be. Opening one particular, very dusty crate, I had my answer. There emerged piles of letters and bundles of paper, all neatly tied up with string.

On top was a note that said: '*These two tin boxes contain my correspondence and documents which might be considered of interest and importance. I hope that these papers will not be destroyed without a duly qualified person examining them.*' It was signed by one E. Cadogan; so bidden by my namesake, I naturally had to look more closely.

As I started to delve into the contents of the boxes I straight away found a group of letters dated 1708-1712. They formed a correspondence between the Duke of Marlborough and the 1st Earl, who had been the Duke's Quartermaster General. I quickly realised the significance of what I was looking at. These crates had probably not been opened for a long time.

Digging further, I soon found Uncle Eddie's papers. (We call him 'Uncle Eddie' but to be precise he was my great-great-uncle Edward, my great-grandfather's brother). They had probably been in the loft since being packed into trunks when forming part of another move, when the family came to Snaigow from Culford Hall in 1934. I doubt if they had been touched since then.

I found this connection to my namesake – another Edward Cadogan – quite poignant. It felt just as though Uncle Eddie was talking to me from the past. I sat down in that dusty, old loft in Scotland and started to read his Great War diary, painstakingly written in his meticulous hand. Four or five hours later, I emerged thoughtful into the night.

Both of us being soldiers the most powerful insight here, as I looked back at his exploits, lay in the striking similarities I found between his experience of war in the past and mine, in the present. I had been in Saudi Arabia, Kuwait and Iraq during the first Gulf War and now, as I read his diaries, I discovered that Uncle Eddie had experienced many of the same thoughts, fears and aspirations in 1913 as I had before going to war 80 years later.

In my own experience, confirmed here, conflict itself feels similar too – often being 90% boredom and 10% intense fear and activity. That was certainly true in the Great War and is still the case.

After five years of transcription, cataloguing and editing, we have put together the story of Major Edward Cadogan's war, both in pictures and in print, as a tribute to the man he was. I hope that you enjoy this diary as much as I have.

Major Edward Cadogan
1880-1962

July 1914 – August 1915

The Pre-War Months

Tuesday, 21st July
Today I received an invitation from Princess Beatrice to ask me to stay with her at Carrisbroke Castle. I replied, rather tongue in cheek, to her equerry that I would come if not garrisoning some east coast town.

Princess Beatrice (centre) and self (far right) during a flower show at Carrisbroke

Wednesday, 2nd July
I went to a ball at Lord Farquhar's house in Grosvenor Square to see the King, Queen and the whole of the royal family. The next night, my father gave a large dinner party at Chelsea House in honour of Prince Lichnowsky, the German Ambassador at the Court of St James. I noticed he was questioning my father very closely and I wonder whether he was trying to find out about the Irish crisis as he must have known my father was very familiar with the Irish problem.

Chelsea House which stood on the corner of Cadogan Place and Lowndes Street

Friday, 24th July
I went down to stay with Lionel Rothschild at his place, Inchmery, on the Solent. The Buckingham Palace Conference has definitely broken down. There seems to be nothing for it but civil war in Ireland.

Saturday, 25th July
This afternoon we went out on Lionel Rothschild's small sailing yacht. It was a dull, calm, hazy day – one of those days when you feel there is something ominous in the air – calm before the storm. I had a conversation with one of his ship's crew who had previously served on the *Meteor*, the Kaiser's great yacht. He told me the Kaiser knew nothing whatever about sailing. We returned to Lionel Rothschild's house to find he had received a telegram from his office in the City saying that the European situation seemed easier.

Monday, 27th July
I returned to London. The government seems to be endeavouring to devise some expedient to extricate itself from the consequences of the disgraceful turn of affairs in Ireland. At about 12 o'clock I was writing quietly in my room at the Speaker's Secretary's

office when, without warning, the door burst open. Morrell, the train bearer, almost fell into my room with a report to the effect that the amending bill regarding affairs in Ireland was to be postponed.

Every moment was of importance if disaster in Ireland was to be avoided. I asked Morrell if any reason had been given. He had not heard of any so I conveyed the news to the Speaker who was seated at his writing table. He snorted and without looking up continued at his occupation. Obviously he attached little importance to the rumour. A short while afterwards he came into my room and informed me that the report was quite true, but he could not adduce any reason.

I accompanied the Speaker in procession into the House as usual. I then walked through the division lobby to the back of the chair where I found Sir William Scott Robertson, MP loitering. I asked him if he knew why the amending bill had been postponed. He replied 'Haven't you heard? There is a regular bombshell from Europe.' In a few minutes we were listening to Sir Edmund Grey's measured words, slowly realising that war might be upon us at any moment. The crisis came upon us so suddenly. Even those in authority had, until this moment, been ruefully unaware of the gravity of the situation.

James William Lowther, 1st Viscount Ullswater (1855-1949), Speaker of the House of Commons

Saturday, 1st August
I went for a walk in the Row. War looks almost a certainty. I sat down on a seat to collect my thoughts. I had not been there long when the Prince of Wales came riding by attended by young Althorpe. They pulled up opposite to where I was and the Prince signed to me to come and speak with him. He told me that the news was serious and that a very bad telegram had been received the night before. He asked me what my brother Willie was going to do. I could only say that I was sure he would rejoin his regiment when it returned from South Africa. I then walked over to the Bachelors' Club convinced we were in for it. I sat down at once and wrote to the Adjutant of my Yeomanry to ask him that if he was making out a list of Suffolk Yeomanry officers volunteering for active service at the front, to include my name.

In the afternoon I went down to White Lodge – a grace and favour dwelling – to stay with Lord Farquhar, who was Lord Steward to the King's Household. I found the Farquhars and my sister all very agitated. On Sunday, Prince Arthur of Connaught had telephoned for Lord Farquhar about tea-time to say that there was bad news. The Cabinet had met and decided to remain neutral. I don't know whether Prince Arthur was merely repeating a rumour or whether his information was from an authoritative source. If it was, then it was obvious that Asquith was convinced that he had the people with him. My brother-in-law, Sir Samuel Scott, arrived from London with grave news concerning mobilization. It was obvious now that nothing could save the situation.

Later on I went for a walk with my sister along that lovely oak avenue which is visible from the windows of White Lodge. Our conversation was solemn, consisting of predictions of what was to happen to us all in this overwhelming crisis.

Sunday, 2nd August
I returned to London with young Cecil Green, Lady Farquhar's grandson, who was starting his examination for the Diplomatic Service that morning although he had no idea whether or not the examination would be held.

London is intense with suppressed excitement. We are always a phlegmatic people and never more so when there is good reason for being otherwise affected.

Tuesday, 3rd August
I heard Sir Edmund Grey's statement to the House of Commons. When he came to read the King of the Belgians letter making his supreme appeal to England, I knew that not even the Liberal government could make a mistake as to the right course to pursue. While I was behind the Speaker's chair I overheard a conversation between Asquith and my brother-in-law as they were leaving the Chamber. The latter was enquiring of Asquith how soon the Territorial Army would mobilize. 'It mobilizes automatically with the army' Asquith replied. I know what I am in for. I went into the Speaker's study and had a few words with him. I told him that I should probably be off at once with my Yeomanry. I then went into my office and had a conversation with the staff before taking my departure.

Returning to Chelsea House I found Willie in great fettle – as all soldiers should be at the outbreak of war. He told me that one of his amusements during these days of waiting for his regiment to arrive in England has been going round to White's Club listening to the elderly *habitueés* there talking big about the war ... 'It will be over in a week' and so forth.

Wednesday, 4th August

I dined with Duncannon and Frank Goldsmith, who is the MP for my home constituency – the Stowmarket division of Suffolk – a great friend and incidentally, my Squadron Leader in the Yeomanry. We decided to perambulate the streets to see what we could see. Crowds were everywhere and we went down to Constitution Hill to the space in front of Buckingham Palace. It was densely crowded. Some of the younger population were swarming up the Victoria Memorial. I have never felt so insignificant in my life – just one of a vast crowd that would soon be scattered hither and thither all over the world at the mercy of events. It was getting near to eleven o'clock – midnight by Berlin time – when our ultimatum to Germany would expire. If no answer is received we will be at war.

As Big Ben strikes eleven the King and Queen come out onto a balcony amid a burst of cheering the like of which I have never heard before. They both wave their arms then turn back into the Palace. The Prince of Wales, who accompanied them, lingered for a while then waved his arms again eliciting further cheers from the crowd. Afterwards we pursued our way round into Birdcage Walk to see the guards preparing to depart in the courtyard of Wellington Barracks. Then I left my companions and returned to Chelsea House. It is a hot night and my windows are wide open. I lie in bed and I can hear the perpetual rumble of the military wagons coming past the house, doubtless from the Hounslow Depot. It is the army mobilizing and the thought of it sends a thrill through my system.

Duncannon, Walter Guinness and Frank Goldsmith. Duncannon on the right of the backseat and Goldsmith on the left, with Walter Guinness at the wheel

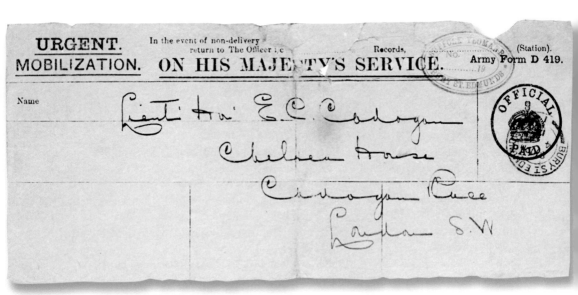

I joined the Auxilary Forces in 1907 (Suffolk Yeomanry). On 4th August, 1914 I was mobilized with my regiment. We were sent to the east coast of Suffolk when a German invasion was expected. We remained in the neighbourhood at Woodbridge for some months

14

Thursday, 5th August
It was past 8 o'clock and I was shaving when my servant brought me an official letter containing my own mobilization orders. They were to the effect that I was to report myself at Bury St Edmunds at 9.30am on pain of the severest penalties if I failed to do so. Hurriedly I flung myself into my uniform, went down to my father's bedroom and asked him if I could borrow his motor to take me to the station. After breakfast I returned to my sitting room to settle a few urgent matters. Willie came in to say goodbye. He told me he was going out with the expeditionary force in the capacity of King's Messenger. His regiment was on its way back from South Africa and he was going to rejoin it as soon as it returned.

I caught the first train I could to Bury St Edmunds. My squadron was mobilizing as best as they were able with a hopeless deficiency of most essentials. I stayed the night with my brother officers at The Angel Hotel.

Friday, 6th August
The first difficulty that confronted us was our lack of horses and therefore our first assignment was to scour the neighbourhood asking those who possessed a stable to give up as many horses as they could spare. It was a distasteful assignment, but there was such a universal scare in Norfolk and Suffolk that a large German invading force would soon be occupying the sacred soil of England that the inhabitants of East Anglia were prepared to make any sacrifice to ward off the damage. In fact they looked upon us, and others who were being mobilized locally, as the only protection against the invaders.

The Culford stables[1] provided three horses, two of which I appropriated as my own chargers.

We spent the next few days in high spirits having plenty to do of a practical nature; being busy with the likes of drafting horses and collecting transport etc.

My charger

1 Culford Hall was the Cadogan family's country home.

Tuesday, 10th August

We received a telegram ordering us to hurry on to Ipswich as fast as we could. It did not matter how unprepared we were for any emergency. I thought that these orders were rather ominous. We paraded on Angel Hill in front of the famous old Abbey gate and as we turned out on to the Ipswich road Frank Goldsmith, who was riding by my side, turned to me and said 'We are going away for three years.' To this I laughed, it seemed too incredulous.

We were within a mile of Ipswich when a motor cyclist met us and told us that we were to serve out a hundred rounds per man and then report on arrival to the cricket field just outside the town. We arrived there just before dusk and found the rest of the regiment with Colonel F. Jarvis, who was in a great state of excitement. We were told to wait for further orders. The Colonel told me there was a strong rumour that the Germans had actually landed. This sounded like active service. We waited hour after hour in the dark. I grew tired and lay down to snooze under a hay stack. At about three or four in the morning we were told we could retire to our billets.

Wednesday, 11th August

Edmund Green, Hodgson, and myself are all in the same billet. We arrived at four in the morning and were greeted beautifully by the good ladies of the house in their dressing gowns, thankful to have troops billeted upon them in protection from the invading host.

Thursday, 12th August

We were told to parade in the self same field where we had dismissed at the end of our armed training in May. A curious incident occurred as Hodgson and I, with our batmen, were proceeding to our objective. Hodgson suddenly realised he had left his sword behind in camp so he sent his batman back to fetch it. The batman was riding towards our billet when he reached a gate by the roadside. He dismounted, tied his horse to the gate, put the muzzle of his rifle in his mouth and blew his brains out.

We remained at Ipswich for several days during which we endeavoured to discover how many of our men would volunteer for active service overseas. All the officers did so at once.

Tuesday, 17th August

We received orders to move off to Woodbridge.

Walter Guinness, Frank Goldsmith, Edward Greene and I, all lived together at Woodbridge during this period of inaction, in a small, new brick house just above the Woodbridge Grammar School. We lived very happily together and in relative comfort. Our camp was in a field nearby. We spent most of our time training on Martlesham Heath and its neighbourhood. I was the Troop Leader, which was mostly composed of yeoman farmers. Living cheek by jowl with them I got to know them well and to be devoted to them.

The Bryn, our billet at Woodbridge

Edward Greene and I

*Sentry over
our camp*

B Squadron, Suffolk Yeomanry, 1914

On exercise at
Woodbridge

Sitting room
at The Bryn

Guard training at
Woodbridge

Wednesday, 25th August
I was woken at four in the morning by a bugler sounding the alarm outside our windows. I rushed down to the stables and made my men ready. We were then ordered to move down to the coast. It turned out that this was a false alarm given to us for practice.

Sunday, 30th August
I went over to Culford for a day's rest. There I found one or two guests staying there with my father, one of whom was Lady Wolverton. We sat on the lawn and listened to the startling report describing the retreat from Mons; it was a depressing tale.

Culford Hall

The following week I went with my troops to Felixstowe, where every sort of extravagant and fantastic defence scheme was being described, including knocking the fronts out of houses.

Shingle Street is the place on the coast where it is thought the Germans have selected for landing. We often went down to site trenches in the shingle.

The whole time we were at Woodbridge we were subjected to a series of demands from the expeditionary force in France for more horses, more officers and men. Increasingly our non-commissioned officers were given commissions and posted to other regiments. Most disheartening.

Trenches at Shingle Street

On exercise on Bronswell Heath

Kit inspection, B Squadron

A demonstration in cooking by 'Click Tooth'

The condition under which the army is fighting in France is horrendous and the casualty list of friends and relatives is growing. It is now noted in correspondence and in the press. I have an uneasy feeling that it is wrong for us to be living a life of comparative comfort and ease and security while the army on the Continent are suffering such tribulations.

Every now and then there is some indication that our brigade might go to the front. One day we had orders to be inoculated, on another we had orders that our transport was to be re-organised. But no, Kitchener has no further use for us yeomanry yet.

September

I have been appointed Assistant Adjutant of my regiment, which means that I have to supervise the musketry and I have to spend day after day on the range at Bronswell Heath getting recruits through their examination. I'm expected to turn out a completely efficient rifleman in too short a space of time. I regret to say that I occasionally cook the score. I have every excuse: I know it is all important that we should have more manpower in the expeditionary force which is, at this point in time, in the most precarious situation.

Our ordinary troop drill is alternated with field days. I've had the chance to go to London once or twice this month. On one of these occasions I met Willie in town. His regiment was then just on the point of arriving in England. Just before I left he came to say goodbye to me. It was the last time I saw him alive.

Friday, 13th November

I was just coming in from drill with my squadron when a motor cyclist flashed by us and went on up to our billets. I cannot account for it but I had a very strong portent that this was ill news. When I reached my lodging I found a telegram. Willie had been killed at Ypres the day before.

For weeks past, every time I've opened the newspaper I've read of all my old friends and schoolfellows being killed. Here is the crowning blow.

Immediately I hurried up to London. My father is absolutely stunned.

Thursday, 26th November

I returned to my regiment to find that the Essex Yeomanry has been ordered to France. Our brigade consists of the Norfolk, Suffolk and Essex Yeomanry – under General Hodgson. This decision appears to us very insidious and we are all very indignant at not being the elect.

Our stable lines, Woodbridge – in the muddy season!

Instructions for
barricading roads
against vehicles
which may lead
Zeppelins to
Ipswich

SUFFOLK YEOMANRY.

No.1 POST.

Railway Bridge on IPSWICH – WOODBRIDGE line over
BRAMFORD – IPSWICH Road.

2nd Lieut. C.B.A. Jackson, 2 N.C.O's and 8 men
report here at 5 a.m. with reports for Nos. 1, 2, 3 and
4 Posts.

No.2 POST.

Railway Crossing on by-road WESTBOURNE to IPSWICH
2 N.C.O's and 4 men.

No.3 POST.

Railway Crossing WHITTON to IPSWICH.
2 N.C.O's and 4 men

No.4 POST.

Railway Crossing DALE HALL to IPSWICH by-road.
2 N.C.O's and 4 men.

No.5 POST.

HENLEY to IPSWICH Railway Crossing
2 N.C.O's and 4 men.

No.6 POST.

WESTERFIELD to IPSWICH Railway Crossing
Lieut. Hon. E.C. Cadogan, 2 N.C.O's and 8 men.

No.7 POST.

TUDDENHAM to IPSWICH Railway Crossing
2 N.C.O's and 4 men.

At 5.15 a.m. at No.6 Post Motor Cyclist will call for
reports from Lieut. Cadogan.

The weather has taken a turn for the worse. We've had incessant rain and the mud in the stables has become awful. This we've attempted to remedy by heaping gorse on the top of it, which is the only way to keep it under any kind of control.

Tuesday, 8th December

At last a little improvement in our lives; they've built us proper stable huts with concrete floors. Life at Woodbridge is tedious. There seems to be no immediate chance of our going abroad. We settle ourselves down and reconcile ourselves to this dull routine.

Sunday, 3rd January, 1915

I'm awoken in my billet near midnight by the sound of a gun being fired. I look out. There is a whirring noise in the air. This turns out to be our first Zeppelin raid! We receive orders to at once stand to our horses. A more idiotic order could not have been given. As it was, if a bomb were dropped, the whole regiment might have been wiped out. Thankfully nothing of this sort occurred.

King Edward's Horse had recently taken the place of the Essex Yeomanry in our brigade. But within days this regiment had orders for France. Jack Seely commanded them. He told me that he had been out in France recently where he found everyone wishing to be back in England. Here in England everybody wishes to be in France.

I've received promotion. I am now a captain and second-in-command of A Squadron. There are one or two officers in that squadron who are thoroughly disgruntled as I have been put over the head of one particular officer who had previously been senior to me. However, he had left the regiment a year or so ago, thus forfeiting his promotion. I told the officer concerned that I sympathised with his grievance and that I was prepared to, in the interests of good feeling amongst the officers, ask the Colonel if I could stand down in his favour. The Colonel would not hear of it. So again I consulted the officer and appealed to him to behave loyally to myself under the circumstances. He is failing to play the game. This makes things very difficult as I find myself with a clique of officers who take his side and resent my coming into the squadron. It is all very unfortunate. Moreover I am very sorry to leave my old troops and they're sorry too. They presented me with a gift in token of their esteem.

General Sir Walter and Lady Evelyn Guinness with General Hodgson

February
Drill and training has become terribly tedious. It is somewhat relieved by very pleasant weekends spent at a place called Sutton, an attractive house standing on a hill above the river which Walter Guinness has taken with his wife Lady Evelyn. I've been going there most weekends. It is delightful at times to be quite alone except for one's host and hostess. Always in a regiment one longs for solitude occasionally.

Saturday, 20th February
What a fine afternoon! I spent it wandering alone in a pine wood. I flung myself down on the turf looking up at the blue sky through the trees and wondering what is going to happen to the world and how it is all going to end. For an instant I experienced peace – for a few moments the world could get along without any assistance from myself.

5th Earl Cadogan

    We've succeeded in getting in a few days' shooting, mainly at Campsea Ashe, and we've started a pack of drag hounds which is rather enterprising.

Friday, 26th February
I learned today that my father is seriously ill. Not a surprise, he has been failing in health for some little time, but a shock nevertheless. An operation had become necessary after which he rallied somewhat.

Friday, 5th March
I had gone into Ipswich with some brother officers to have supper. In the middle of which I was handed a telegram saying that I should leave for London at once as the latest news of my father's health was precarious. I at once hired a motor and set out for London. The journey through the night seemed endless. At last I arrived at Chelsea House late at night. I went straight up to the bedroom where I found my father unconscious and sinking rapidly. I stayed for a few moments by his bedside but it was obvious that he was beyond recognising any one of us. So I went back into the next room and waited until the end.

Friday, 6th March
The end occurred at 2.30am.
    As I gazed upon my parent for the last time there came a surge of remorse into my heart. Regrets that on so many occasions and for so many reasons we had not understood each other better and that up to the hour of his death I had done little enough worthwhile to the family's credit which could have made him proud of my performance. On the contrary I must have been a perpetual source of disappointment to him. But keenly as I have felt these regrets, it was some consolation to me to reflect that I had never once given my father any cause for anxiety.

We laid my father to rest by the side of my beloved mother in the family vault, which he had built in Culford Church. After a few days' leave I rejoined my regiment.

When I returned to Woodbridge I found the life of a camp was ceasing to have any attractions for me except that I was occasionally in command of A Squadron. The added responsibility rendered the routine more interesting.

Saturday, 24th July

I've a weekend's leave so went up to Culford to spend it with Jerry – my oldest brother and now the 6th Earl Cadogan – and my sister-in-law, Marie. And very interesting it proved to be. General Smith-Dorien, the hero of the retreat from Mons and of the battle of Le Cateau, was the only other guest. After dinner he produced his maps. He gave us the most vivid description of the retreat from Mons. He told us that the original expeditionary force consisted of only 90,000 effective units. At Le Cateau he had received a signal from General French 'Go on retiring, do not fight.' Smith-Dorien wired back to say that his men were too exhausted to retreat any more but they could lie down and fire. Hence the stand at Le Cateau and hence probably the salvation of our army. He told me that the reason the Germans turned away from Paris was on account of the concealed army in the vicinity. I am completely fascinated and inspired by General Smith-Dorien. He is a brilliant military leader.

Monday, 26th July

Today we moved to Leiston, a small village near the coast. It is delightful being near the sea.

Tuesday, 3rd August

The regiment was reviewed by General Smith-Dorien. Gradually the omens are moving in favour of our being sent to one front or the other.

Thursday, 19th August

I am very much enjoying my time here at Leiston. A sentiment I think shared by all in the squadron. I regularly take them down to the shore. Bathing on horseback is a delight to experience. The horses seem to enjoy the novel sensation as much as we do. The only drawback, if one can call it such, is that one has to be careful when dismounting to prevent the horse treading on one's instep. Much as I love horses I have come to the conclusion that they are the clumsiest animals in creation. The obvious precaution against such a contingency is to wear shoes and yet such an expedient would detract from our centaur-like appearance. Never before have we looked so heroic, so Olympian, as when bestride our bare-backed horses in a complete state of nudity. I must explain that the stretch of sea coast where we indulge in this activity is remote and closed to the public.

Bathing at Leiston

Frank Goldsmith returning from Aldborough with the news that we had received marching orders for the Dardanelles

The first intimation we received of our marching orders came when I and a few officers of my regiment were dining in our mess tent one evening in September. We heard a motor cyclist buzz up and stop short just outside. Crisp, who was Orderly Officer, went to see what was required, thinking it was the usual alarm of Zeppelins. But we heard the orderly saying that he had brought more important news than a threat of an air-raid. I made a bet, which I subsequently won, that it meant our departure from these shores. About an hour later Frank Goldsmith returned from Aldborough, where he had been out to dinner. He was in a great state of excitement and told me that we had received marching orders for the Dardanelles and that Hugh Buxton (our Brigadier's ADC) had motored to Aldborough and had given him the information. But this was inaccurate. The real message, I found out next day, was to this affect. From the War Office to the Brigadier: 'Is your brigade prepared to go dismounted to the Mediterranean?' – Goldsmith's message however was good enough for us. My first feelings were those of keen excitement and pleasure. I went down to the men's camp that night and spread the good news. There were wild cheers and everyone, with a few exceptions, seemed pleased. I was thoroughly disgusted the next morning when a sergeant (I regret to say in the squadron to which I had just been transferred) came to me with chattering teeth and asked me to take him to the Colonel to have his commission papers signed. This would mean a respite for him of another six months in England! He was in such a hurry to get out of the regiment that he got hold of the wrong form and the Colonel could not sign. He subsequently had to come with us to the boat as his gazette was not out in time to prevent his going with us. I must say I had no use for such as he, and afterwards had occasion to wish he had been given his commission.

For the next few days I felt extremely relieved that we had been given our marching orders. We had been playing at soldiers long enough. The Brigadier at once answered the War Office that we were prepared to go anywhere and do anything.

26

The first outward and visible signs of our equipment for the East soon appeared in the shape of pith helmets and drill jackets. Jolly smart the men looked in them too!

Crops of rumours began at once to circulate in camp, nearly all inaccurate. We commenced a strenuous course of training, part of which I was delighted to get out of – I had had quite enough training. My name had been sent in for a course of explosives at Godstone in Surrey and thither I took my departure two or three days after our warning orders had been received. I did the course comfortably from Chelsea House, except on the two or three nights when we had night trench-fighting, when I was billeted on Sir Frederic Kenyon (the Curator of the British Museum) who had a small cottage in Godstone. The course was interesting. I had to learn the new scheme of taking trenches with a grenadier party both by day and by night. Also, I was taught how to make bombs and throw them – dangerous amusements for the novice. We were given plenty of demonstrations with high explosives. These took place in Marsden Park and Fosterdown Fort. It was during this course that I had my one and only experience of a Zeppelin raid on London. I watched it from the top windows of Chelsea House. I never heard such a row. I imagined that the whole of Piccadilly must be in splinters, but the next morning on my way to the station a policeman told me that the bombs had fallen miles away in the City.

My course continued until the 18th September. It wasn't a bad experience. The Commander was a sapper called Gillespie who had met Willie at Chambra in Kashmir, and he was very kind to me as a consequence. At the end of the course I spent two quiet days' leave in London. I collected some bits together. Unfortunately, while buying a compass, I met a wounded Australian from Anzac in the shops who told me I should take nothing out but what I could carry on my back. I foolishly took his advice. My advice to soldiers proceeding anywhere on active service is: take as much as the authorities will let you and a great deal more if possible. You can always throw away what you don't want at the front, whereas you can't make up for a deficiency there.

My kit

Mounted tug-o'-war

Sports at Woodbridge

Leiston, August 1915

Troops filling their paliasses with straw

Out riding

Tuesday, 20th September

I returned to my regiment at Leiston. Everyone seemed to be taking the whole business quite calmly – all seemed to be in readiness for a move. We did nothing much until Wednesday morning when we paraded for General Broadwood to bid us farewell. Poor man! I remember his talking to us about how when we had broken through to the Hungarian plains we would get our horses back!

Up to this moment we had received no definite orders – so typical of the War Office. At length they arrived. They were to the effect that we were to leave at an early hour next morning for an unknown destination. That night I went to bed early in order to get as much sleep as possible – but Frank Goldsmith frustrated this plan of mine by tramping up and down on the floor above me. We had rented a small, empty cottage as our tents leaked so abominably. I eventually dozed off but was roused from my slumber by Frank Goldsmith's batman who was almost as noisy as his master. It was about 3 o'clock in the morning. I got out of bed feeling calm and collected. Having put on my uniform I struggled into my pack for the first time, and covered with haversacks, water bottles, field glasses, pistols etc. – until I could hardly move, I strolled out into the dim morning light to the camp where the cook had come up to scratch splendidly and had provided us with the best breakfast that could be

Frank Goldsmith, 'Apples' and General Horne

contrived so early in the morning. About an hour later we paraded and were marched down to the station by the 6th Suffolk band. My pack and other things began to tell by the time we reached the railway. It was rather a dreadful scene on the platform. All the wives had insisted on coming and the result was distinctly distressing. I got into a carriage with my squadron officers and we started on our journey to Liverpool. We passed through Bury St Edmunds. Branwell Jackson produced some champagne which made my folding cup stink of stale wine for the rest of the war. When we ran through the slums of Liverpool all the windows were crowded with cheering people, which put the heart into us again. Another painful march of about a mile when we left the train brought us to the Alexandra Dock where we were drawn up and told to wait. While doing so I observed the Colonel with some maps; there were some of Egypt and some of the Dardanelles. It began to rain.

"We are fighting for a worthy purpose and we shall not lay down our arms until that purpose has been fully achieved."

SUFFOLK YEOMANRY CAMP,
WOODBRIDGE.
December, 1914.

Given by Frank Goldsmith to all members of B Squadron to commemorate the formation of B Squadron

Dardanelles – Gallipoli

Editors' notes:

The British force sent to the East comprised troops destined for the Dardanelles, Egypt and Mesopotamia.

By 1915 there was stalemate on the Western Front. Both sides were heavily entrenched on a front line which stretched from Switzerland to the North Sea. There were no further outflanking manoeuvres possible. It was argued that a new Eastern Front might be opened. An idea was conceived that would knock out Turkey – the weakest member of the Axis Coalition – and help Russia. If the Dardanelles were under allied control this would afford access to the ultimate goal of Constantinople and open up a route into the Black Sea.

The Dardanelles is a narrow strip of water linking the Mediterranean, via the inland sea of Mamora and the Strait of Bosphorus, to the inland Black Sea. Initially, taking control was attempted via inadequately planned and badly managed naval offensives.

After two failed attempts, a combined naval and ground offensive was undertaken. Troops were landed on the Gallipoli Peninsula. By September, 1915, fighting had been ongoing for several months. Reinforcements were being continually drafted in.

Unbeknown to them as they waited at the Alexandra Dock, the Suffolk Yeomanry, with Edward Cadogan as one of their number, was on its way to reinforce the Gallipoli front.

After a while we were told to march by squadrons to the ship. Up to that moment we did not know what sort of ship it was. One rumour had it that it was to be one of the ships of the Navy. I am glad it wasn't. HMS *Terrible* was used later for this purpose and was known by men who had the discomfort in travelling in her as the *Bloody Awful*.

Our transport was the *Olympic* (sister ship of the ill-fated *Titanic*) a leviathan of some 46 thousand tons. When we were drawn up opposite her berth I noticed that her name was painted out, an unnecessary precaution I should have thought in view of her appearance. As we arrived alongside, Guy Benson rushed up and greeted me. He is on the brigade staff. It took our regiment two or three hours to get settled into the ship. Men were abominably crowded, located in the first-class dining saloon which had had all the decoration boarded up. It was a curious sight – the inside of the *Olympic* rigged up as a troopship – an object lesson in contrasts. There was a florid looking ladies' boudoir turned into an armoury. All the porthole glass was painted black as a precaution against submarines. A great deal of sackcloth covered the walls. I shared a most comfortable cabin with Edward Greene. Curiously enough it was the identical cabin which Edward had occupied when he had travelled in the *Olympic* to America a year or two ago. Some of the generals and officers had the most gorgeous apartments; a mass of priceless carving and panelling. It was much too much of a contrast with the filthy quarters our men were provided with. Our food was luxurious and in great abundance. Our men were absolutely starved. Pryor, who occupied one of these American millionaires'

Edward Greene on the Olympic

cabins, told me an amusing incident. Two of his men were looking in through his porthole not realising he was in the cabin and he heard one of them say to the other 'Poor devil! He has got to share this with someone.' Our men's hammocks were almost touching each other, crowded together by hundreds in the most evil-smelling atmosphere imaginable.

There were nearly 7,000 souls on board our ship. Rather too many eggs in one basket. I found plenty of friends and acquaintances. There were eight Members of Parliament: Peter Saunders, Winterton, Sammy Scott, Harold Pearson, Gilbert Wills, Frank Goldsmith, Walter Guinness and Duncannon. The Upper House was represented by Camden, Sackville, Kensington, Hambleden, Vivian and Guildford. There were three Generals: Hoare, Clifton-Brown and Hodgson. Among friends outside my regiment were Con Benson, Bear Mills, Percy Thelluson, Chops Ramsden, Slug Marsham and Denzil Fortescue. We had a Members of Parliament dinner one night to which I was invited as Speaker's Secretary!

We did not start on Thursday, and Friday morning still found us in the Mersey. Then news went round that as it had become so generally known all over England that the

Olympic was starting on Thursday, no less than 150 telegrams arrived with the name of the boat correct. This shows the harm that silly babbling officers who sit in the War Office might do to us if the worst consequences of their indiscretion were to result.

The authorities are now very afraid of submarines in view of this indiscretion and Saturday morning therefore finds us still in the river mouth. We had a parade at 9.30am on that day (we had not been allowed to leave the ship for a second) and just as we are forming up we see three destroyers approaching us from the direction of Liverpool. As they pass us we begin to move and a signal comes from one of the destroyers: 'If there is a submarine at the mouth of the harbour I will run up a green flag.' I should have thought it would have been the last place in the world to find a submarine, but I suppose the Navy knows its own business. When we were just clear of the harbour mouth, all of a sudden the three destroyers commence going round and round in very small circles, the bows of one almost touching the stern of the other. I presume they were using some sort of depth charge. Then one of them signals: 'Just give us another five minutes.' While this was going on we are at a standstill, but when the destroyers get straight again we moved off and proceeded down the Irish Channel on a very tortuous course. I am told we are not going more than 19 knots. I can well believe it. We did not make Holyhead until 3pm although we started from Liverpool at 10am. I think we must have cruised about the north coast of Ireland in our efforts to avoid the dreaded submarine. It is most curious the way our escort turns and twists about. We had an alarm drill this afternoon, a most tedious but necessary affair. The

Suffolk Yeomanry machine gunner on the look-out for submarines

One of the Olympic's *destroyer-escort*

Suffolk Yeomanry on the Olympic

ship has run short of fresh water. As evening closes down we are given the strictest instructions not to reveal any lights, not even the business end of a cigar is to show itself on the deck after dark. After dinner, when it was as black as pitch, our Captain signalled to one of the destroyers what the *Olympic* looked like and if she were showing any lights. 'Your ship looks like a floating gin palace' came the reply! I suppose doors and portholes had been left open everywhere. Everybody is wearing patent inflatable waistcoats, which even when not inflated accentuate the figure. Some of our *Apollo Belvederes* (and there are several on board) do not look their best, but safety comes before appearance on these occasions. Our escort left us at the Scilly Isles with a message wishing us all luck. Very kind of them I am sure, but I had sooner that they came with us to see what sort of luck we were going to have.

Sunday, 27th September
Hopeless muddle about church parade – only room made for a few of the troops to attend. While parading for this purpose I had a bit of a turn. I suddenly saw the gunner forward preparing to fire his gun and a moment later he had loosed it off. I looked anxiously for a periscope but it was only a trial shot. The OC announced today that we were under orders to go straight for Lemnos. We were now in the Bay of Biscay and the sea was getting rough. All the troops were sick everywhere indiscriminately. We tried signalling classes morning and afternoon but the sea was very rough and I was one of the few who stuck it out. I went down to the men's quarters in the evening at tea-time. I have never seen such a sight or smelt such a smell. It was a ghastly beer garden; the sick men's hammocks were hanging just over the tables and everyone was being sick all over the place. On all the companions and everywhere were traces of *mal de mer*. It was a very high test but I stood it without a qualm. There is not nearly enough food for the soldiers and the man who looks after the condenser deserted before we left Liverpool, so there was a deficiency of fresh water. I started censoring the men's letters, a new sensation which they didn't like at first but soon got used to. I often think it would save an awful lot of trouble and almost do good to let the men write what they like. They are so nearly always wrong that the enemy would never know what to believe, even in the remote contingency of any of these letters ever being seen by an enemy.

Monday, 28th September
The gymnasium is a great stand-by on this ship and so is the swimming bath. In the evening I learn from Jack Agnew that we are to land at Mudros. We may stop there 48 hours or we may be hurled straight on to the peninsula. We heard good news by wireless of the advance on the French front.

Tuesday, 29th September
This morning we were not yet in sight of Gibraltar, we were evidently going well out of our course on purpose. In fact we began steaming down the coast of Africa in the afternoon as our orders were we should only go through the straits at night. In the evening came stringent instructions to close everything down and to put out all lights. I went on deck as we passed through. A brilliant searchlight played upon us from Gibraltar and a signal was sent asking the Captain what our ship was. 'Ask the Admiralty' signalled back our Captain. It was a lovely night. I took a look at the dark coast where Tangier stands and thought of the happy days I spent there years ago with Gerard Lowther and Charlie Meade.

Wednesday, 30th September
Quiet and peaceful day in sight of the beautiful coastline of North Africa. Passed a coastal town with gleaming white houses – gorgeous yellow sand in the background.

Friday, 1st October
All preparations for going straight up to the front on the morrow. At about 3 o'clock we sighted two lifeboats drifting about, full of people. The Captain stopped the *Olympic*, contrary to all orders. It was a mad thing to do as these boats could so easily have been a decoy and even if they weren't, we should be a glorious target. Besides which, all he had to do was inform the nearest harbour by wireless. He was endangering the lives of 7,000 for a handful of evil-looking Greeks. They have got the French flag. With difficulty they are hauled up the precipice bow side of our giant vessel and our machine gunners use their boats to practice on. The rescued ones explained that they had been submarined at 8 o'clock this morning. The crew of the submarine had told them that if they had been English they would have killed the lot. About two hours after this incident, just as I was coming up on deck, I heard a shot from one of our guns and shouts of 'Submarine!' Then the alarm system sounded; a series of short hoots, which froze the marrow in one's bones. We all went to our stations and donned our lifebelts. I tried to blow out my patent waistcoat but it wouldn't fill so I discarded it in favour of the old-fashioned belt. General Hodgson found one of the crew trying to pinch one of our belts. He took him by the scruff of the neck and shook him like a rat. The men all behaved very calmly. Soon after the signal was given, the *Olympic* began to keel over at a terrible angle so much so that I began to wonder whether we had been hit and that what I thought was our gun might have been a torpedo. But as a matter of fact what had happened was the Captain was trying to turn the boat round on a sixpence. It is marvellous how these vast ships can turn. I daresay that manoeuvre saved us from a great disaster, as the submarine, after

firing two torpedoes at us, passed us to starboard. It was the mercy of God that no submarine came across us earlier in the day when we stopped. With 7,000 souls on board the disaster that would have ensued is too terrible to think of – but it was a prize worth having for the enemy. We waited at our stations for a time. While doing so I noticed, on looking over the side, that a large number of portholes were open. I asked the Colonel if I might go down and help to shut them, which I did accompanied by Sergeant Green of B Squadron. When I got down below I found a naval officer engaged on this job. He seemed in a bad temper. I said I hoped they wouldn't shut the water-tight doors while we were doing this. He replied grumpily 'Well it can't be helped if they do!' I daresay not, but he needn't have been so short about it. We steamed in the opposite direction for some time but as there were no more excursions and alarms we eventually made for the Aegean. Barring such incidents, such as the above, our life on board was pleasant enough with glorious Mediterranean weather.

I remember, one day as I came up the companion steps, finding poor little Osbourne sitting at the top supremely happy and contented. He had been arrested for disobeying orders but the orders that he had disobeyed were that he was not to go to the front. Two or three years later he died in the thick of a battle on the French front, being recommended for the MC for great gallantry.

Mudros from the Olympic

Saturday, 2nd October

Heard that we passed two men swimming in the sea this morning. How terrible it must have been for them seeing us pass by on the other side. When I went out on deck after breakfast there was a fog so we had to slow down and blow our siren and, as it was in the danger zone, I felt we must be giving ourselves away – to say nothing of rocks as we were in among the Greek islands, which seemed a trifle compared with submarines. The mist cleared at midday and we came into Mudros harbour at about

1pm. I was standing on one of the upper decks as we came in sight of this famous island. Poor Harold Lubbock was standing beside me. I heard him say 'What a God-forgotten spot!' I must say I thought I had never seen a sight so superb as that which we were then gazing upon. The sea was the colour of *eau de nil* – the hills a hazy blue and the sky cloudless. A silver airship was circling over our heads.

The harbour was magnificent and rendered most lively and interesting with the numerous and varied craft of all shapes and sizes. All sizes, but none equalled ours – we towered out of the water above them all like a Titan amongst minnows. Men-of-war, transports, and hospital ships all yielded in impressiveness to ourselves.

The General at once put off for orders. There were none. They didn't seem to have expected us and it looked as if we should have to wait for some days.

It was a glorious night and all the men collected in the well deck of the ship where we had an excellent sing song under the stars. The Welsh Horse, who were brigaded with us, were the *pièce de resistance*. How those rough miners can sing. I never heard anything so perfect. They went through a repertoire varying from *Lead Kindly Light* to the latest comic song – all sung in parts and it was difficult to say which was most beautiful.

Sunday, 3rd October
Service in the morning. Disquieting intelligence by Marconi to the effect that Sir Edmund Grey announced in the House of Commons that German officers were going into Bulgaria. Here the message jammed; presumably it was jammed by the enemy. Dudley and Granard came on board but I did not see them.

Monday, 4th October
News about Bulgaria confirmed – so now it looks as if we are in the soup. Pleasant news as a send-off for us before going to the peninsula. How can we hang on in there with Bulgaria against us? Thousands of rumours everywhere. Went on shore with General Hoare, a silly, brave lunatic of a man who always thinks he knows better than the experts. He took charge of the gig and utterly declined to go where the Petty Officer assured him there was a landing. He preferred his own course and we stuck in the mud some yards from the shore and we had to make a bridge of planks to land. Thank goodness I am not serving under this General anyway. Once on dry land we went for a walk. Met with an old Greek on a small donkey, General Hoare put his finger to his ear and gave the most piercing 'View halloo'. The old man just looked up and made a gesture as much as to say 'Your General is off his head anyway.'

The island is very arid with a mass of encampments everywhere. I talked with some British Tommies who had been on the peninsula. They had had a quiet time of it of late but there has been a great deal of dysentery. When we went back to our ship I saw three transports leaving harbour.

Tuesday, 5th October
Nothing much doing.

Wednesday, 6th October

During morning parade Tomkin comes along the deck and says that we have got orders to move in two hours' time. Military authorities love moving troops in two hours' time. Troops hate it. The Colonel is on shore and so Walter Guinness sends for all officers and announces that we are off to the Dardanelles. We all get ready at once. The men get their packs on and then when we have fairly set the whole machine in motion we are told that our orders are cancelled until the day after tomorrow. It seems that all military orders have to be cancelled once at least! I remember my regiment getting an order to hog our horse's manes. When we had done so an order came for us to un-hog them. In war you must never believe that anything is going to happen until it does and then you have to pinch yourself to make sure you are not dreaming.

As I was strolling about deck in the afternoon while the ship was coaling, I suddenly heard my name called out in a hearty voice and looking round I saw a naval officer quite unrecognisable as his face was black with coal dust. This I discovered to be Alistair Graham who asked me to dine with him on the *Lord Nelson* where I spent a very pleasant and very different evening to what I thought earlier I was going to do. Alistair apologised for the discomfort of his ship. I envied the comfort of it. He said they were cleared for action. They had put away the silver photograph frames and snuff boxes but otherwise it might have been The Ritz. Sailors have a much more comfortable time of it in war than soldiers. They have magnificent cabins and clean sheets and whiskies and sodas to return to after the night watch. The soldier after his turn in the trenches lies down hungry and thirsty in the dust, or mud, as the case may be.

Thursday, 7th October

Today one of our brigades left with Sammy Scott amongst them. I am told I am to be in reserve at the base for a bit as I am second-in-command of the squadron. I protest and get my protest up to General Hodgson, who says he will do what he can to get me on to the peninsula as soon as possible. Delivered a bomb lecture in the evening. Alistair Graham comes to dine with me on the *Olympic* and gives us the bad news that Bulgaria has definitely come in against us. Yesterday General Mahon left with the 10th Division for Salonika but returned today, no-one knows why. Percy Thelluson was his ADC. He came on board and told us they had gone towards Greece but had had to return, I presume for political reasons. Every day I see a beautiful white ship going out to sea to bury the dead.

Friday, 8th October

Up at 5.30am to superintend our men drawing their iron rations. Had to sit on a court martial at 9am, procure brandy for my squadron officers – a most necessary medicine out here, and lunch with them at 12am and then go and see the regiment on to their boat which is drawn up alongside – a most melancholy business. Back I go to the ship and watch them from one of the lower decks. All of us who are left behind with reserves hate it and an awful thought strikes me that one is in a position of contempt, although not one's own fault. This thought becomes unbearable as I see the boat sheering off. I rushed up to A Deck across the well deck and right up to the bows where I stood nearly alone waving to my regiment. They all cheered back and I felt better. I shall never forget the extraordinary contrast of the bustle and noise of 7,000 men getting ready in the morning and the emptiness of the afternoon.

Saturday, 9th October
Heard that the poor Suffolk Yeomanry, owing to the rough sea, did not reach their destination but had to lie to somewhere. I feel so anxious for them. We get orders this morning that all the remaining units are to leave the *Olympic*. A sort of penny steamer comes alongside about midday, and although we were supposed to have all been off at three, we did not leave for the shore until after five. It was an awful business. Our penny steamer took us very slowly across the harbour to an improvised jetty where we disembarked. The sun had set and so we had this difficult operation to perform in the dark with no chance of getting up to the camp, which was about five miles away over difficult country. They told us not to take off our heavy baggage as the boat would remain alongside until the next day, so, nothing doing, we struggled on about 300 yards and bivouacked on a small sort of peninsula. We ate what

Suffolk Yeomanry disembarking for Gallipoli

provisions we had with us. I had brought half a bottle of champagne from the *Olympic*. It was a glorious starlit night and the harbour looked brilliant. We lay down to rest on the ground but were knocked up at 12.30pm with the news that the boat had been requisitioned and that we must get all our heavy baggage off as soon as possible. So for hours we struggled in the dark. Campaigning is made up of such incidents as this, which do not read as great hardships but which, when totalled up, make life difficult to bear. The regiment cleared the baggage off the boat, another ran it along in trolleys and a third stacked the beastly stuff. It was a scene of indescribable confusion.

Sunday, 10th October
After scarcely any sleep I had a tiresome morning waiting about for orders to move up to camp. These came at about ten and then we saddled our packs and marched away across the island. But it was hot and our webbing and equipment, unaccustomed as we were to it, did seem heavy. We stopped once to rest by the roadside and as we were doing so Alistair Graham came by looking spotless in white ducks accompanied by two middies (one being Glenconner's boy). They were going up into the hills to shoot partridges. How I envied them. There I was sitting in the dust by the roadside, sweating away with all my worldly goods on my back and there they were going partridge shooting! The luck of the Navy! They looked so cool and happy compared

Our camp on Mudros

to ourselves. It was a frightfully long trudge to camp but at last we found it on the west coast of the island – in a lovely situation looking towards an awfully pretty bay, but I felt dreadfully depressed. I was parted from so many friends in my regiment. I had had little enough sleep and a terribly hot march. All the news we had heard of the European situation was most gloomy and I felt less keen than I had felt since the beginning of the war. There were tents in our camp. I shared mine with three brother officers; Barker, Quin and Leslie. Walter Guinness was next door, fretting terribly about being in reserve. A few friends in other regiments were sharing the same fate – Eddie Winterton, Bear Mills, Slug Marsham and Jack Camden. Eddie Winterton in great form.

The water is very short here, and, on the first day, so was the food, but our batmen concocted a splendid stew for us which, although was composed of curious ingredients, tasted delicious. In the back of my mind is always the wonder of how the regiment is faring. A beautiful night so I sleep outside my tent. In the small hours I am disturbed by rifle fire in a neighbouring village. I was told afterwards it had got something to do with an escaped prisoner, or the departure of Greek reserves – same sort of thing I suppose.

Monday, 11th October
Today we spent chiefly in getting the camp ship-shape but I had a delicious bath in the evening with Eddie Winterton. We took our men down to the bay. A man was drowned although not while I was there. My depression is leaving me. The flies are awful.

Tuesday, 12th October

Violent headache. In the evening a Colonel Fortescue arrives saying that he has heard all the details – we are to be off tomorrow morning early. Walter Guinness is away foraging for food in the villages so I have to give instruction to my regimental details. Fortescue thinks we are going to Egypt. Walter returns in the evening very pleased to be away from here and I must say, the prospect of remaining here does not altogether please me. I pack what there is to be packed – not much, and turn in pretty soon but spend a disturbed night with the three brother officers, one of whom snores, the other coughs and the third talks in his sleep.

Wednesday, 13th October

Walter Guinness calls us at about 6am with the intelligence that we are all off to Anzac. This does not dismay us very much. We are told we have got to move out of camp by nine o'clock. No *contretemps* in getting ready except that my water bottle appears to be leaking, a serious matter in these parts – luckily this proves to be not so. We serve out our men with iron rations and gas masks and then start off on our long dusty march to the harbour – a fine day but blowing very hard. Walter Guinness gets a letter from Edward Greene in which he says the Suffolk Yeomanry failed to land the first night as it was so rough. A man on board their boat was killed – not one of our men – as they approached the shore.

After some delay we proceed onto the most miserable little boat I have ever seen but I am relieved to discover that this is only the tender to take us out to our boat in the harbour. Our boat turns out to be an old mail ship, a sort of Dover to Calais boat, only not so big – comparatively comfortable. To our joy we found lunch on board as we were aching for food. At 2.30pm we fetched up alongside the *Aragon*, the GHQ boat, of bad reputation – much exacerbated by taking too much care of itself and not enough care of those at the front. I met Jack Crossley on board, one of our officers who left the regiment as soon as we were given marching orders and went on the staff. I shouldn't so much blame him only this young gentleman in peacetime always posed as such a hero. I found out where his cabin was and before leaving pinned a note to his pillow, telling him he simply must come to the Dardanelles. He never did. The luxury on the *Aragon* was proverbial and I should think the administrative staff that lived on her was one of the worst imaginable. Whether Kitchener dispensed with them when he came out or not I do not know, but I expect they were all covered with DSOs and mentioned in all despatches.

At 4pm we started punctually on our wonderful quest. The wind was a head one so we did not feel it. We had a most excellent dinner in the saloon and it was difficult to get out of one's head that this was just an ordinary channel crossing and we were ordinary travellers. Up on deck there were certainly signs of war. The metal was riddled with the marks of shot and shell. I expect these tubs had had a part in the original landings. But any illusions that we might have had so far were dispelled when an officer came down to the saloon and said that all lights must be put out. He left us with a sort of night light. We had been cheery up until that moment having had a good dinner and then a feeling of melancholy came over us. I went out on deck and saw a long, low coastline beginning to appear. This was Cape Helles. As we neared it you could see sudden bursts of light here and there which presumably were shells bursting or guns firing. After keeping up along the west coast of the peninsula for some while, although some way out at sea, our ship began to slow down and now we were opposite what, from the blaze of lights, seemed a town like Margate nestling under high, rocky hills. I was standing by Walter Guinness when we came to a stop. We were still some way out from the shore of Anzac Bay. A curious and acrid smell was in the air. I had been told you could smell Anzac some miles out to sea. The smell was chiefly due to the innumerable incinerators, but I daresay there were plenty of other causes. When the paddles of our steamer stopped an incessant fusillade of rifle fire could be heard all over the land. Close to us a destroyer suddenly started shelling. It was the first time I had ever heard a shell fired in anger and I was much impressed. Walter said that these were only small shells but they made a noise like a motor bus going through the air. The whole scene was weird and impressive to a degree. For months I had read of the desperate tenacity of the British Army in the Dardanelles and here was the British Army before my very eyes still holding on by the skin of its teeth to that narrow strip of shore which its deeds of valour had made famous for all time. After some delay, an armoured lighter comes out of the darkness and draws up alongside us. Walter Guinness and I collect the Suffolk Yeomanry details together and shepherd them on board this peculiar craft. The whole ship's load of them are then packed like sardines into it. Yeomanry and Indian coolies all together and we wonder what it will feel like if a few stray bullets come on board. However they don't and we buzz off to the jetty. I am detailed to be the first officer to land and make my report to the MLO. When we come to a full stop I jump out, very nearly falling into the sea doing so, and grope my way in the darkness to where I can see a small lantern on the ground. This I find belongs to the MLO who is standing by it. He seems to have expected us as he says there are two guides waiting for us so I went back to Walter Guinness and together we got the men out of the sardine tin and drew them up on the beach road. The guides turn out to be two men from the Suffolk Yeomanry. They start off with

Suffolk Yeomanry packed like sardines on the way to Anzac

Anzac Beach

great confidence to pilot us. They give us the welcome information that all is well so far with the regiment and that we are to go up to the rest camp for the night. I might explain that the word rest was only a comparative term on the peninsula! We are being conducted along a sap of immense length with high parapets on either side as it is quite easy to get badly shelled here, when we begin to suspect our guides are not at all certain of their way. We came to where the sap divides in two directions on a sort of forked road and one of them says we had better wait here until he has ascertained for certain which is the right prong of the fork. We wait a long time. He does not return so we come to the conclusion that he has lost himself. Walter Guinness and I then decide there is only one thing to be done, namely to return to that beastly beach for the rest of the night. We pass some dug-outs but their inhabitants don't seem to know the geography of the place and cannot help us – so we find ourselves back in Anzac cove. When we got back to where we started it was 2am. We found a very kind Colonial in a dug-out by the jetty who telephoned up the next morning to try and find out where our regiment was. He crouched over the telephone with a candle by his side, pretending there was a girl operator at the exchange and saying to the signaller at the other end 'Say, you've got a very bad *gurrl* at the exchange, you must get a new *gurrl*.' He was very kind to us poor lost souls and allowed us to doss down just outside his dwelling, facing the sea so we could get some protection from the stray bullets and any chance shells that might come our way.

It was bitterly cold lying out on the ground and I got no sleep. The rifle fire on the cliffs a few hundred yards above us was incessant. The destroyer lying off Anzac

Scaling the cliffs above the beach

Achil Dere, Pemberton in foreground

bombarded in the most deafening manner at intervals. Trains of mules kept passing (and re-passing) us, almost treading on our feet. Every now and again bullets winged through the air over our heads and landed with a plop in the sea. I was not exactly miserable. All the sensations were new and therefore more stimulating than depressing.

When day had thoroughly dawned, our colonial friend telephoned up to Headquarters and the reply came that a guide would be sent down to us. He turned up in about an hour's time and led the way. We discovered *en route* that if only we had proceeded last night we were on the right track. It was a terrible walk along a sap uphill: carrying all our kit was a great exertion. On the way up the Achil Dere we met Evelyn Pryor and he gave us an account of the place. We live, he said, with an incessant sound of rifle-fire and shell-fire in our ears. Every square inch of the ground is potentially under fire and one is always liable to get overs day and night. At length we arrived at our camp which looked like an enormous pit, horse-shoe shaped, with the dere running out of it at the bottom end. It was known as Bedford Gully. To get to the top of the sides of the pit was certain death and even inside it only one flank of it was protected – the other side was in full view of the enemy and doubtless had machine guns trained on it. I was told the enemy had not yet discovered we were inside it and they had not yet shelled the place. Blencowe, our *padre* gave me breakfast. As I sat eating, three rifle bullets whizzed over my head. I was told I would soon get used to that sort of thing. Most of the regiment were up in the trenches not far from here and I was told to wait for orders. I spent most

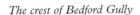

The crest of Bedford Gully

Bedford Gully

Rifle inspection before going into the trenches

of the day making my dug-out safe (comparatively speaking). There is no riveting material so you cannot really make a dug-out safe. Our food, I find, is decidedly simple. It consists of bully beef, bad water boiled, and jam (always apricot). This I supplement with a little brandy I have brought with me. I hope to learn the wrinkles as to how to get something more appetising later on. The flies are awful. I slept the night in Frank Goldsmith's dug-out, which is a very bad one with no head cover. Incessant firing all night. Bullets whizzing overhead. If they come at a certain angle they make a noise like a cricket bat hitting a ball. It sounded exactly like somebody was practising cricket in the gully all night long. There are graves all over the place. No lights are allowed so we have to turn in at about 7 o'clock which is most depressing.

Friday, 15th October
The dug-outs in this gully are very scarce and they are extremely necessary if you are to rest. I really believe these so-called rest camps are less restful than the trenches, but there is not much peace anywhere in the Dardanelles.

This morning I went to see my squadron in the trenches – my first experience of trench life of which I have read and heard so much. I met Pemberton who showed me round. This particular line of trenches was comparatively comfortable as it was over 1,000 yards from the enemy. It commanded the most beautiful view and we were far enough off to look over the side in safety. They were very narrow and deep and seemed to be made of clay which crumbled rather easily. Our men seemed in good spirits. Sickness and other troubles have not yet begun. One of them asked if I would like a shot at some Turks he could see. I fired away and instantly there was an angry message on the telephone from a digging party of ours out in no man's land that my bullets had gone close to them! After going the rounds I returned to Bedford Gully where I met Jack Agnew who had got a telegram in his hand from General 'Joey' Davis asking me to go on his staff. I refused without any hesitation because I considered it such a rotten thing to do to leave your regiment when you go out on active service for the first time. I think everybody ought to try the front line if they can. If they cannot stand it then I don't blame them so much for going on staff, but everyone should test themselves, and I wanted to do so now. Jack told me that we had all got to tuck ourselves well into our dug-outs tonight as there was going to be a great demonstration on the British side all down the line, of firing and shooting. This, of course, would put the wind up the enemy and our gully might come in for a heavy shelling.

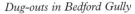
Dug-outs in Bedford Gully

A typical Anzac trench

Saturday, 16th October

Woke at 4am when the bombardment was supposed to begin but I did not think it was anything very terrific. I went off this morning with Walter Guinness to see the trenches of the 1st Australian Division at Anzac. They were the show trenches of the whole place – known as Lone Pine. We had to go down onto Anzac Beach, a wonderful place to see, a hive of industry with all its munitions and provisions being landed and despatched up to the front line. We proceeded round by Hell Spit and up a steep hill to the right, the site of one of the most heroic battles at the beginning of the campaign. The Lone Pine trenches were a wonderful sight. I have never seen such labyrinthine tunnels, galleries, turrets and saps. It reminded me somewhat of the gun placements in the rock of Gibraltar. These are old Turkish positions, and there are piles of Turkish bodies buried in the parapet of the trench behind sandbags. There was evidence of this. In one place the sandbags had burst and what I saw had better be imagined than described. One of the peculiarities of the Lone Pine trench was its proximity to the enemy. One often hears of trenches in France being a few yards away from the enemy, but at one point the Lone Pine trenches are contiguous to the enemy's positions. The Australian who was showing me round said at this point 'You see that sandbag wall; the enemy is just behind it.' They used to bomb each other at first over this wall but I think both sides had come to an understanding about it. However, my guide asked me not to talk while we were passing this fragile barrier. The Australians I saw in these trenches were men of fine physique and were cheerful lads. I had excellent views through periscopes of the Turkish positions. One I looked at did not seem to be more than 20 yards away.

On coming down the steep path towards Hell Spit the enemy started shelling with shrapnel, a good many of which went into the sea. We continued our way until we got to the beach. Walter Guinness was walking in front of me. A piece of shell whizzed down within a yard of us and made us jump – much to the amusement of some Australians on the beach who made light of these things. I was very thankful to get into the sap. When I got back I went to the A Squadron trenches where they told me I had been attached to the 5th Norfolk Regiment for instruction. Their trenches were next door to ours, so I went and reported myself to them in their dump which was just behind the front line. I found the officers at mess. Their dug-outs are in a lovely situation on high ground facing the sea with a fine view of Imbros and Samothrace in the distance. I prefer this to our rest camp. The Adjutant to the Norfolks – Eustace Cubritt – was awfully kind to me and I share a dug-out with him. I took a tremendous liking to him at once. He is one of those rare men you feel you could go anywhere with – he was so calm and collected with a very keen sense of humour. He never seemed down in the mouth. He was in the original Suvla landing. He told me he had had an awful time and had lost his two brothers on that occasion. He was a most charming fellow and I wish I had been with more of his sort during the war, but there are not too many of them.

Met Gibbs. I heard to my infinite regret today that Charlie Mills, Miles Ponsonby and Tommy Robartes had all been killed on the Soane. Gibbs, our Brigade Major, told

Suffolk Yeoman resting in the trenches

me this news in one breath when I met him in the morning in the Lone Pine trenches
– such news makes one very depressed.

The 5th Norfolk mess is a delightful one – the officers are a very good lot of fellows
but they have suffered terrible losses in this regiment and it does them great credit that
their pecker is up still.

Sunday, 17th October

Had a good night's rest in this most comfortable dug-out and wake feeling much
refreshed. I have got a ledge on one side of it, Cubritt on the other. He is very good
value as a companion under these circumstances. I went and did a turn in the trenches
this morning – went into them again at night but there was nothing doing. There was
a brilliant moon. The evenings and nights here are certainly very beautiful. There
always seems to be a lull in the firing just at sundown – perhaps it is the Turkish hour
of prayer, but the effect of it is very peaceful. The peninsula is full of birds and it is
refreshing to hear them singing unaccompanied and not to the perpetual rifle fire. At
night under the moon the effect of the whole place is picturesque. On the sea the most
noticeable feature is the hospital boat with its brilliant row of green lights the length
of the deck and the illuminated red cross.

Coming back to my dug-out I am nearly hit by an over – which are rather
ubiquitous here. The weather changes and it pours with rain all night which does not
add to one's general well-being.

Monday, 18th October

Find the place not nearly so muddy as I expected. The sun in the morning is so hot it
dries the ground very quickly. Do a turn in the trenches then visit my squadron in their

trenches where I find a lot of men going down with dysentery – the scourge of this place. Idle afternoon. In the evening while I was sitting in the 5th Norfolk dump suddenly there was a whirring through the air over our heads and a deafening explosion. The men in the gully had been, up to this moment, laughing and shouting. There was now a dead silence for a second or two and then a shout of 'Stretcher bearers!', a cry that gives a shock when heard for the first time. We had had a dose of shrapnel but only one man wounded.

Tuesday, 19th October
We move down to what they please to call the rest camp of the Norfolk Regiment, a horribly exposed place. We have got much worse dug-outs than up above and we are treated to some very nasty doses of shrapnel in the afternoon. I rejoined my squadron today. We hear that Ian Hamilton has gone and Munro has taken his place. As a matter of fact this happened some time ago but news percolates slowly up these gullies. It leaves an unpleasant sensation on our minds, this bowlering of the Commander-in-Chief. It cannot mean that all is well. Our meals down in this dump are very badly run and we have got nothing to eat. I am much struck here with the extraordinary calmness of everybody under adverse circumstances, although the majority are very melancholy. I have got a very bad dug-out, very unprotected from weather or shells and I find it almost impossible to fix a waterproof sheet over my unfortunate head. I manage somehow and after an apology of a supper crawl into my rabbit hole, light a talk lamp and read *Pickwick* – the only book I have brought with me. Nobody seems to have got any literature at all on this peninsula and as parcels seem to mis-fire the prospects for the library are not cheerful.

Norfolk Yeomanry rest camp – a horribly exposed place

Wednesday, 20th October

A man was wounded by an over close to my dug-out this morning. Our Brigadier comes round to see us. The first words he addressed to me were 'Nice game for cavalry men isn't it! And the worst of it is one sees no end to it.' Tomkin, my Squadron Leader is ill so I did not like to go far afield in case I might have to take charge of the squadron. General Godley comes up to see Tomkin (who was his brother officer once) and we three sit together in a dug-out. Godley was most interesting. He is a magnificent specimen of a soldier. There is a tremendous lot of firing tonight.

Thursday, 21st October

This morning the whole of the Suffolk Yeomanry join up in our dump in Bedford Gully. This manoeuvre has its advantages and disadvantages. The chief advantage is being all together, whilst the chief disadvantage is being overcrowded and having not enough food. What there is of it being incidentally nasty. The want of decent food and food of any kind is beginning to tell on us – it is extraordinary what an important factor food is in human existence. I already feel weak whenever I start digging and we are always digging here. Our food consists of small quantities of bully beef, rice, jam, tea and biscuits. The water is very bad indeed and there is not nearly enough of anything. I treasure up an inch of soapy water in my canvas bucket as if it were brandy! Another disadvantage of this dump is the noise of our own bombardments – we have got some of our guns mounted close and the ships fire shells over our heads and the din is awful. I hear Edward Greene has been evacuated with dysentery, a disease which is catching hold of my regiment. Every morning there is a queue of men looking like ghosts standing outside the doctor's dug-out. It is awful to be ill under these conditions. They give stripes to men who have been wounded, but men who get dysentery have just as bad a time. The reason for its prevalence here is that we are so cramped we are obliged to have sanitary arrangements quite close to where we eat and the flies are fearful. These pests must now be very poisonous as there are so many dead bodies lying about just above where we are.

Our dump in Bedford Gully

It is a terrible time at night for those who have dysentery; lying on the hard ground and constantly going across to the latrines in the cold air. Some of them are so weak they can hardly drag themselves there. Most of them are wonderfully brave about it. A good many of them have to be evacuated and sent to Malta or Alexandria but that is generally against their will, it is wonderful the way some of them have stuck it, they deserve any reward for what they go through in pain and suffering. Some of them die of it.

Pemberton asked me whether Bedford

52

In the trenches

Gully was not my idea of hell – I looked round at the place with its innumerable holes for men to lie in and its generalisation of depression, and was disposed to agree with him.

One of the chief occupations of the men when they are not on duty is to search their undergarments for lice which swarm here – some poor fellows are absolutely spotted all over with them. Nearly everyone had them sooner or later, both officers and men, although luckily not myself.

Friday, 22nd October

We hear very bad news from the Balkans and it looks like the Germans will make their way through, but you never know your luck. Up to now we have been keeping cheerful *rebus in arduis*, but it gets a bit hard to be cheerful when one hears nothing but bad news, when our men are going down sick as fast as they can and when the weather gets as bad as it did today. There is nothing to protect you against the weather but Job's comforters and when at the end of the day I went into my dug-out I confess that my heart failed me. It poured with rain most of the night which kept me awake as I was insufficiently sheltered. Heard from Sammy who is at Helles.

Saturday, 23rd October

I awoke this morning feeling really down in the dumps. Everything looks hopeless. The news from the Balkans is as bad as it can be. I feel that if I only could have a good square meal I could cheer up. We spend the morning in digging out a mess room for A Squadron officers. My own dug-out consists of a small niche cut in the clay, a bank

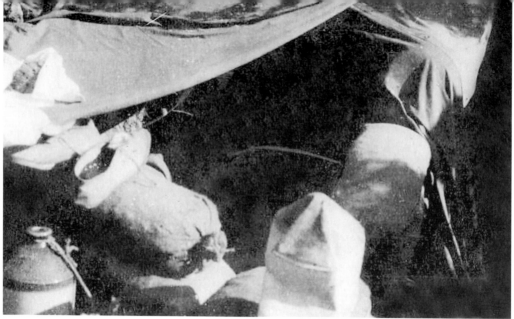

My dug-out

of earth on one side and a few sandbags on the other. There is just enough room for me to lie between the bank of earth and the sandbags. Round my head and sides are crowded my haversacks, bandolier, pistol, water bottle, lamp etc., etc. A mass of earth keeps falling every time I move. Over my head are tied (very insecurely) two waterproof sheets. One of them has a great hole made by a pick right in the middle and is therefore rendered useless, the other is badly torn at the edge and corners. Last night they were not sufficient to cover me entirely and my feet either stuck out in the rain or I had to assume a cramped position. The only redeeming feature of this undesirable residence is the view I get when I scramble out from the waterproof sheets. I look down the gully towards the sea with a lovely aspect of Samothrace. I can see the ship, which is tantalising. I long to be on it instead of this lovely view – a most unmilitary thought. If the news I hear today is true, the Turks may have German reinforcements down here soon, to say nothing of Bulgarians. Although this ought not to daunt us, it does seem

View from my trench

hard that just as the Turk was being worn down they should get an accretion of strength. However, although we seem to be in a bad way, I hope I still have faith that all will yet be well. As a matter of fact it is a curious thing that when you really are in a tight place one does not fuss nearly so much as one might think. It is the anticipation of evil which is always so trying. But oh! For a good square meal.

Sunday, 24th October

It poured with rain in the night and is still raining. Blencowe held a service at 7 o'clock which the Brigadier attended. It was rather melancholy in the half-light of the early morning with a leaden drizzle settling upon us. It was a cheerless day altogether. Bad news from everywhere, including a special message to us from Kitchener who tells us to dig in deeper and be prepared for German shells. But we can't dig in deeper as we

Our Officers' mess, Bedford Gully

have no material to do it with! My squadron seems to have been attacked with dysentery worse than any other. Altogether we are a bright party although our evening meal is always a cheerless one. We have got no candles and we sit around on packing cases in the twilight, brooding over our troubles while bullets whizz over our heads. You read in newspapers and despatches how wonderfully cheerful the men are, that may be so in France, but in the Dardanelles I hardly ever hear a joke or see anybody smile – ever. In our mess Tomkin presides. He generally has a one-liner and his conversation consists in cursing one for eating too much of our all too scanty fare. Pemberton is so dreadfully ill the whole time his conversation is not calculated to inspire and Limmington never utters a word. Jackson is sometimes cheerful, but generally at other people's expense.

I have got a small candle end in my dug-out. It is all I have left in the illumination line. I never thought I should ever set so much store by a candle. I wouldn't part with it for £20 and I would have willingly given £20 for two or three more. My cigarettes are also running short. How I value that wretched bit of tallow. I managed to read a few pages of *Pickwick* by it tonight and am saving the fag end for tomorrow. After that – the dark. To my joy I found tonight that I had got one more slab of chocolate than I had thought to allay my hunger with. Of such importance are such small details now. I regret to say I have sunk so low in spirits that I even envy the fellows going down to the hospital ships. What a wonderful contrast those ships must be to this awful place!

Monday, 25th October
The clouds have disappeared and we woke to a glorious morning. The view of Imbros is lovely. As far as appearances are concerned it is only man that is vile here. It is impossible for the men to keep tidy and clean. I am a great believer in the men keeping up their self-respect under any conditions.

The view of Imbros

Terraces cut out of the sides of the gully

Meet Jack Agnew with bad news as usual of the Balkan situation. Our dump is a wonderful sight in the morning. Bullets whistle through it day and night. A piece of shrapnel fell close to where I was standing this morning. On one side of the gully terraces are cut, and from these terraces the dug-outs lead into the ground, but not far into it as we have got no wood to shore the ceilings up. Cooking operations go on at the lower end. Aeroplanes (German *taubes*) come over us on fine days. When that happens the order is that we should remain still and not look up. Both these orders are always disregarded. However, luckily they never drop bombs and are invariably very high. The life of an officer in the dump is usually a very idle one while that of the men seems to consist of fatigue jobs. They go down to the beach and sometimes get hit on the way. It is a dangerous path. My sentiments at the moment are not very lively. I am so tired of not having any bright prospect to look forward to – it is a sort of heavy, dull feeling of despondency which weighs upon the mind and which action and motion would relieve. It is this dreadful hanging about in one place which is so depressing. A good climate and a good glass of wine would probably set one up again and make the world look a bit more rosy. Also, one lives in such a circumscribed sphere both material and moral. I only see a few brother officers, with whom incidentally, I have lived for a year without hardly a break and so our topics of conversation are dried up and we are getting on each other's nerves. This, I think, contributes as much as anything to the general feeling of melancholy – this utter want of variety both of scene and companionship. I am sure this is so because, for instance, yesterday, an officer called Oliver came up to see me, who used to be a sergeant in my old troop in England and now has a commission in a regiment of the line out here. The effect of conversing with somebody fresh outside one's regiment was extraordinarily cheering and I felt a different man at once. We are all beginning to look dirty and untidy; our clean linen and other such finery is fast running out. I sleep in my clothes every night bar my jacket, partly because it is so cold and partly because one might be called up out at any time. I always shave every morning. I have a miserable India rubber basin with about an inch of water in it, a small bit of sponge and a bit of carbolic soap. I take off my clothes occasionally and wash myself by sections. I feel that this process, which is a farce in most respects, keeps me free of the animal pupae, or, at least I hope it will. Everything gets so nasty, soiled and torn – but I am sure none of these little trifles and petty grievances would annoy at all if only one could occasionally have some good news and some good food. We hardly hear any news at all. Our mails seem rarely to come – it is said because the staff on the *Aragon* are so selfish and inefficient. Apparently it takes five weeks for a private parcel to reach here, which is a cheery look out. Oh! For England and peace! I am not writing quite like a soldier but then was there ever such a campaign as this? On the outside it resembles the accounts I have read on the Afghan campaigns.

I was going to Suvla today to visit Peyton's division with Frank Goldsmith but our expedition fell through owing to there being a Squadron Leaders' pow-wow, so again I spend the afternoon in the dump and in the dumps.

A great deal of shell-fire today from both sides, much more than usual it seems to me – and the eternal machine gun and rifle fire. A curious thing I notice about the shelling here, both from friend and foe, is that every gun seems to shell at the same hour every day. I should have thought it would have been much wiser and more effective to vary the process, but I suppose they know their own business best. Went for a short walk to the Bedford camp in the evening, the first walk I have had out of our gully for five days. Hear a rumour this evening that the Bulgarians are advancing unopposed on Gallipoli. Hope it is not true.

Tuesday, 26th October
Awoke about three in the morning with the prospect of going into the trenches. Am feeling pretty cheap when I hear a shout from Tomkin that it is time to get up. The dump looks rather picturesque in the faint light of very early dawn – it might be a good subject for *détaille* – but I am not in the mood for appreciating artistic effects. In fact I feel about as miserable at this hour as a man could. Getting up at 3am in peacetime is bad enough but in war ... We parade just before it gets light and have a dreary and rather dangerous walk – hung like Christmas trees – up a long sap to our trenches, where chaos reigns supreme. Nobody from whom we take over knows anything. The Dardanelles blight has settled down badly on the outgoing tenants. We find our dump in an exposed place – an officer tells me it was shelled yesterday.

We post our sentries in the trenches and then turn to what food we have, which is not of a quality or of an amount to cheer very much. Afterwards I explore the trenches with Tomkin. It is a longish line.

I go on duty at 1pm and am now sitting in the trenches lunching off very nasty meat and varying the proceedings with writing up my diary. From where I write I get a good view of the famous salt lake (Suvla) and the sea beyond. Shells are being fired over here as usual and a sweet smell of burning scrub comes up to my nostrils – but sweet as it is I hate it – I will always associate it with these dismal days.

I am sitting in the trenches at night. My shift is from 11pm to 1am. It is difficult, sleepy work when nothing is doing. It suddenly strikes me that this is like a chaperone trying to keep awake at a ball!

A good deal of rifle fire and bombing seems to be going on as usual. One of our sentries has got a rumour that the narrows have been forced. I get back to my dug-out by one o'clock. Have to get up again at 5.30am for the stand to which we always have as this is supposed to be the hour when the Turk is most likely to attack – this and the evening – so we all have to be in the trenches ready for emergencies. I return to the trenches at 7.30am. What a life!

Wednesday, 27th October

They are already sending shells over our heads in the early morning. Went round the trenches with General Mudge, a conscientious, painstaking, good and very uninteresting sort of soldier. He is too finicky – worries about little details which should be left to the Sergeant Major to worry about. However, he comes up into our trenches a great deal and is always risking his life showing his red hat to the enemy. This is more than most of the GHQ staff seem to do. They may be brave somewhere else but we don't see much of that here. Saw an aeroplane being shelled. Saw myself being shelled a bit later down in Stafford Gully – a regular shower of shrapnel came over. I suppose the Turks are beginning to get ammunition through from Bulgaria. I ensconced myself in an aperture in a bank of a dere and felt extremely frightened. One piece broke a root a yard or two away from me. Birkbeck, of the Norfolks, came into our camp this morning and said that Kitchener had sent a message to us to say that large supplies of ammunition were going through Bulgaria and that we must expect the same sort of shelling as they had in France! Nobody seems to be taking any steps about it. The Generals continue to talk about staying here all through the winter. We are told airily to dig ourselves in deeper against high explosives, but most of our men have gone sick and there are certainly none to be put on any extra fatigues and we have got no wood or iron to make the necessary improvisations. We must just therefore trust to luck. At its brightest it is a bad business. Today it is very hot, it is blowing hard and the flies have come back to us after the cooler spell – worse than ever. To add to our troubles the General comes up the hill today and tells us we have got to take up our quarters in Stafford Gully – a bad pitch. It is heartbreaking having to burrow into the earth into a new place every night. It is the life of an animal, and a hunted animal at that. Stafford Gully is a deep ravine with a dried-up river-bed at the bottom. The trench line comes down the hill

Sandbag barrier in Stafford Gully

one side, across the ravine is an enormous sandbag barrier and then the line runs up the hill on the other side. In the banks of the river-bed are dug sort of shelves. These are our homes. The latrines are just above the river-bank under fire, and a more disgusting, filthy place could not be imagined. Added to which the gully is shelled morning and afternoon with greater fury every day. However, one must expect hardships out here – we certainly are leading a hard life.

Went to Headquarters this evening in the place of Tomkin who felt ill. Took Limmington with me in order that the Colonel should instruct him as to what his particular task was because he is going out on a patrol tonight. The task was to take an NCO and two men with him and approach the Turkish positions. The orders seemed a bit vague and what the object of the expedition might be was left unexplained. However, he returned safely after having accomplished nothing – the usual result of a night patrol. I returned to the gully to find only the fag end of a bully beef tin and a dirty piece of bread for supper. Have had precious little to eat today. I retire to my dug-out ravenous. A terrific gale sweeps up and covers me with foul camp dust just as I am trying to get to sleep. It is too muggy to cover my head with anything. Just manage to get to sleep about 9pm when Jackson wakes me for my shift in the trenches. Sorely in need of sleep as I am, the trenches tonight are preferable to the dug-out, although this line is not as pleasant as the trenches on the hill. After a few hours on duty I retire to my dug-out. It takes me some time to get to sleep and then it is only to be knocked up for the stand to at 5:30am.

Thursday, 28th October

Feel rather better this morning. My hunger had worn off which is lucky as I find a particularly unappetising breakfast awaiting me. Then I begin to feel brighter, why I hardly know. Suddenly Leonard Avery turns up in our gully from Suvla. He used to be our Yeomanry doctor and is now with the Bucks Yeomanry. The joy of seeing someone from outside – especially he – as he is always, under all circumstances, so cheerful. He chaffed me till I felt rejuvenated and ready for any emergency. How priceless this sort of man is in wartime.

Rest in the afternoon. My dug-out is next to that of the cook who kept up the traditions of the British Army in the swearing line. On duty tonight from 9pm to 11pm. We hear rustling in the bushes close to our trenches which sounds like someone crawling stealthily along the ground. We satisfy ourselves it is not human beings. It is either rats or tortoises, both of which abound here. I think it is the latter. The Turks fire a few shells, which they don't generally do at night. They don't like giving their gun positions away. When I was at the barrier I saw Walter Guinness and Eversden coming back from a night patrol. They had got into a Turkish listening post but had met no Turks.

We had a great disappointment this evening. Avery told us that if one of us would go back to Suvla with him he would give us a fine cake. Jackson went with him and brought back a large box which was supposed to contain the said cake. When it was opened it was found to contain chiefly packing, one pot of jam and a small tin of ham. This may sound like a small disappointment to those who do not know what it is like to be without sufficient food for days, but oh! How I long for cake. Had rather a better night.

Friday, 29th October

General Mudge came along at an early hour this morning up the gully and found us all at our posts as it was the stand to. The smell in this gully is disgusting due chiefly to the stink of government blankets, which I presume are old ones disinfected with something beyond the powers of any microbe to endure.

Overhear the following conversation in the cook's dug-out ' 'Arvey 'ave you been confirmed?' 'Arvey: 'No.' 'Well you can be confirmed tomorrow if you like. I would if I was you.'

In the afternoon I struggled up the hill to the Norfolk Regiment to try and find Cubritt but he was away. I met Pemberton who took me into the trench to show me some dead Ghurkhas who could be seen in most life-like attitudes almost on the crest of Sari Bair. Walter Guinness tied a handkerchief to a tree somewhere in the enemy's positions in a patrol last night. I could see it distinctly.

Talking of dead Ghurkhas, I am told there is a part of our trenches where there are a certain number of unburied dead bodies just in front of our parapet and that the enemy turns machine guns on to these bodies so as to make it unpleasant for us. We live in a civilised age!

Saturday, 30th October

The usual restless night. My shift in the trenches from 11pm until 1am, the stand to at 5am – the result, but little sleep. Wander up the hill in the morning to see Pemberton and Limmington. Glorious weather up there and a lovely view of the ships and the sea which I often gaze longingly at. A certain amount of shelling, but none comes quite our way. This evening, after dark, Pemberton goes out on patrol towards the enemy's trenches. I went out tonight for the first time into no man's land. I wanted to see our listening post, which is about a quarter of a mile in front of our line and between ourselves and the enemy, who is about 800 yards away. I got hold of Sergeant Nunn (who used to be in my troop) to guide me out there. I passed out by the barrier. It is an eerie feeling getting into no man's land after being so long in the trenches. It was a dark night and there was a good deal of wire to be negotiated. We got to what looked like a road. Nunn said he knew the way but I noticed he was hesitating a good deal and we were in an exposed place and if a star shell went up we should be a target. I told him firmly that he must either find the way or we must retire and that I did not propose to stand very long on a road in full view of the enemy. However, by dint of guiding himself by the telephone wire we eventually found our way and reached our destination which is situated on a very steep hummock in the valley. It is a sort of crow's nest which we man with one NCO and six other ranks. The reliefs, of course, always take place at night and they are there for 24 hours, the idea being to keep a sharper lookout on the enemy's movements than one can get from the firing line. There was nothing to see as the night was so dark. I could not help feeling as I left them that they would have a sticky time if the Turks chose to attack, and I can't work out why the Turks don't shell the place to blazes. Did a shift in the trenches after I had returned – from one to three in the morning. Our pitch is a very bad one called Hammond's Hope up to which there is a very steep trench by way of approach. Very difficult to negotiate even in dry weather, and, I should think, unscalable in wet. When you get to the post there is not room to turn round. Our other two posts are near the barricade down in Stafford Gully, where one can see nothing. Dividing two of the dark hours of the night between these posts is not particularly amusing. The nights are very fine and still now, with a bright moon. I retired at 3am for a short rest and was roused again by the 11th London Regiment who have come in to relieve us. They are of very poor physique and very young, which speaks badly for recruiting in England. Half these boys ought not to be here at all.

Sari Bair

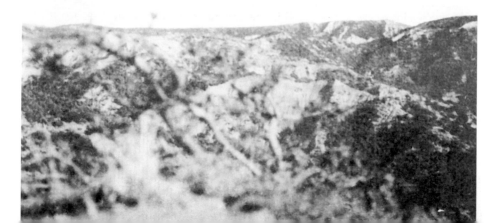

View from our trench crossing no man's land

Sunday, 31st October

We return to Bedford Gully much to my relief. Five days in the trenches is enough at a time. Find that the Norfolk Yeomanry have been occupying our dump and in our absence have much improved it. My Squadron Leader has chosen another dug-out so I appropriate his. This is the seventh dug-out I have inhabited and certainly the best. In the afternoon Frank Goldsmith and I walk over to Suvla Bay, a distance of about five miles, to see Tony Rothschild. The road, down which we start – the Achil Dere, is much exposed to the gaze of the enemy but has a few screens, made of branches, hung across the worst danger spots. There is one bad place called Shrapnel Corner, a most unpleasant spot where a man was killed a few days ago. The custom is to run for it past this corner or you'll probably get it in the neck. We wended our way through the Ghurkha camp and then unto an interminable sap parallel with the sea. All this part is very much under shell-fire. Along very nearly the whole length of it are Indian encampments. When nearing Suvla we come upon the Scottish Horse. Tullibardine was there but his batman told me he was asleep in his dug-out so I did not disturb him. On we went to the Bucks Yeomanry, who have got the oddest quarters situated in a plain not far from the coast. From a short distance away you would not know there was an encampment there at all but when you get close you discover a maze of trenches which wander about the plain and constitute their living quarters. It was these that became so terrible in the cold weather when they were flooded out and men died of frostbite and exposure. We found Tony Rothschild, Leonard Avery and one or two others. They gave us an excellent tea. While we were eating this a shrapnel shell burst uncommonly close. Nobody seems to be enjoying themselves, but they have got orders for Egypt, lucky devils. We returned in the evening in time for a short service which was rather impressive, our camp being a very good setting for it.

Feel the better in mind for my expedition. Change is everything here.

Our front line trench

Monday, 1st November

Wake very early and find I have the prevailing complaint but I soon get better of it. Brighter news from the Balkans. Walter Guinness tells me that the General has been up to say that Greece and Romania may well come in with us. If that is so, our life will be much less depressing here. Barker, one of my brother officers, has been over to Lemnos and has returned with masses of food so, thank goodness, we shall at last have something to eat. Hardly any home parcels have arrived at all. Better news and better food will be powerful antidotes to our melancholy. But alas in the evening I hear that this morning's good news is all bunkum.

Tuesday, 2nd November
A quiet morning. A squadron mess is rather too small an affair. Six human beings must get on each others' nerves a bit leading this kind of life, especially as our conversation consists mainly of disputes as to how much jam or condensed milk each of us ought to take. Also, as far as I can see, ours is the worst run mess of the three. However, we have now made ourselves something of a mess hut and best of all, we have at last got a small supply of candles – the greatest luxury in these parts.

Wednesday, 3rd November
A very dull day. A good deal of sickness about. Weather good – which is a great consolation.

Thursday, 4th November
In the afternoon walked over with Tomkin to Stafford Gully to take over from the 11th London Regiment. As usual, the other regiment that occupies your trenches does nothing to improve and generally makes it much worse, especially the 11th – they are such a poor, undersized, starved looking lot, I shouldn't think they could do anything if they wanted to. I find that my dug-out, for some unknown reason, has had all the sandbags taken away. Return to Bedford Gully. While at mess in the evening I get orders to go up to the Bedford Regiment trenches to see a trench catapult working, in my capacity as bombing officer. I go up there in the dark and report myself to Colonel Brighton of the Bedfords, a swaggering, hairy-headed sort of man, and we enter the trenches. Our shots from the catapult seem quite effective and we believe that we got two or three shots into the Turkish trenches, which are about 150 yards away. Got back to our gully at about 11pm. A good deal of firing going on.

Much improved dump

Friday, 5th November

Got up at 4am feeling very gummy and not at all looking forward to Stafford Gully. However, Walter Guinness comes to my dug-out and says that Frank Goldsmith is so bad with dysentery that I have got to take over the command of B Squadron which pleases me thoroughly. It is the squadron I have always been in up to now, ever since I joined the Yeomanry. So I take up the command and proceed to 'King's Own Avenue' – the habitat of B Squadron, which seems an improvement on Stafford Gully. Not very much, as a matter of fact. It is no easy job to take over a squadron suddenly with the squadron Sergeant gone sick and ditto a great proportion of the officers and men thereof. I spent most of my day learning the geography of the trenches. While resting in the afternoon a couple of shrapnel shells burst in our gully and wounded one man, why they did not kill a lot I don't know. A tremendous lot of high explosive shells came over us but burst a good long way below us on the beach. I think it was the most noisy afternoon we have had yet. Spent from 6pm to 10pm this evening in the trenches. Heard Turks working away in a gully not far from us. I was nearly hit by an over.

Shell-fire

Saturday, 6th November

Had plenty of sleep in Frank Goldsmith's dug-out, the sides of which keep crumbling in on top of me. Stand to at 5:30am then hand in my trench report to Headquarters. After breakfast go up to the trenches. Enter post 17 which is about 100 yards from the Turk, and get hold of a periscope to have a good spy. A Turkish sniper fires at my periscope and hits it. I get a small shower of fragments of glass and metal in my face

66

and hands. Jolly lucky I did not get any in my eye. It felt like somebody hitting me in the face with a cricket bat. Bled profusely and going down through the gully with my face and jacket bespotted with blood my men think I have been wounded. Go down to the first aid dressing station at the bottom of the gully. The doctor takes as many of the splinters out as he can see and makes me look an awful type with patches of iodine and antiseptic gauze all over my face. Walter Guinness asks me if I would like to have my name sent down as wounded. I said certainly not.

Two more officers have gone down to hospital: McKelvie and Musker, making four in all. Dysentery still continues. Weather lovely – perhaps that is the cause of the sickness. It will cause more casualties I am thinking.

Sunday, 7th November
Up at 3am in the trenches. Fire the trench catapult at dawn with a cordite bomb (near Post 16) to Turkish trenches, which are about 100 yards away. Walter Guinness observes for me and says I am short of the mark. While off duty, one of the men comes to me and asks me to go back to the trenches as young Walker has been shot in the head at the same post where I had the *contretemps* with the periscope yesterday. I go up to see him. He is able to walk to the stretcher but is groaning a good deal. I walked by the side of the stretcher down to the dressing station. He eyed me curiously and asked me if he was badly hurt. I tried to reassure him. It may have been the last coherent sentence he ever uttered as his wound was a bad one and he has been a helpless lunatic ever since. He was one of the nicest and pluckiest boys in the regiment. He could have had a commission at any time he liked, but he said he had made his pals in the ranks and he would prefer to go out with them to the front. He was a great loss to us. I hear from Frank Goldsmith who is in hospital down on the beach. He says it is filthy but he resisted the temptation of being evacuated off the peninsula, which was placed before him. He has a very stern sense of duty and would never leave anyone in the lurch.

Plenty of shells this morning over our trenches and dump. I cannot help smiling inwardly when I remember a month ago at Lemnos anxiously and curiously trying to catch a sound of the guns in the Dardanelles. I need not have been so anxious; a month on end of the sound of shot and shell is quite enough to satiate even the most martial mind.

I find being a squadron leader more interesting than being second-in-command. There is more to do – one can make work for oneself, and work is essential under these conditions. Doing nothing will wear away the strongest nerve. It strikes me now that modern warfare is either monotonous or terrifying – it is never enjoyable. The monotony is intensified here as there is such a small area to walk about in, but on the other hand, I am bound to confess I prefer the monotony of the shells!

I took the midnight shift in the trenches so I had but little sleep.

Trench periscope

Monday, 8th November

Much colder this morning. In a spare moment I am writing a description of my kit which up to now has proved, in most respects, sufficient. I have a large canvas sleeping bag – inside it are three Jaeger blankets sewn together, also a loose government blanket, an air pillow and a woollen cap comforter. It is in this sleeping bag my spare clothing is wrapped when on the move. I have a thick, waterproof coat with a double-breasted, detachable, Jaeger lining. I have a private's web equipment, consisting of ammunition pouches, which I use for revolver bullets, compass, etc. My pistol is fixed into the webbing. A small haversack hangs at the side containing shaving tackle and the like – I carry a pack on my back which contains cigarettes, food, electric lamp, Kodak, writing materials, change of linen etc. It is wonderful how much a pack will hold. I also carry an extra haversack with dubbing, soap, knife, fork and spoon and other necessities. Hung around my shoulders are my binoculars, water bottle, map case, mess tin and gas mask. I sometimes carry two waterproof sheets and an entrenching tool. I have a *valise* with extras, both of clothing and other essentials which I leave at base camps. The things which I can particularly recommend as being useful for any degree of comfort while campaigning and which find a place in my haversack when I can procure them are: plenty of chocolate, a talk lamp with a supply of candles, cardigan woollen waistcoats, a rubber basin, plenty of string and small leather straps (the latter invaluable), fly net, compressed spirits of wine with a Tommy's cooker for boiling sharing water, bootlaces, a number of small notebooks, pencils, envelopes, matches or flint lighter, a housewife, a small case of medicines, safety pins, a woollen balaclava helmet, and carbolic soap. With regard to garments I have very few – one suit of drill, one of khaki, two pairs of boots, two sets of putties, and about half a dozen of each item of underlinen. Really with these supplies one could attain a certain degree of comfort if only there was more water. I ought to have more tinned food and a pistol strap.

Blencowe, the *padre*, has just been up to tell me that Kitchener is coming out here to take command. I feel glad about this as we have felt a bit neglected lately on this front and this might mean that we shall, after all, cook Bulgaria's goose for her. News is much better from the Balkans.

Tuesday, 9th November

Did the shift in the trenches from 3am to 6am. Eversden calls me and tells me a Turk came within about 20 yards of our trenches at 2am. My post fired upon him but with apparently no result. Hear that a man in my squadron who had dysentery, was shot in the stomach while lying in the tent hospital on the beach. This is the second sick man from my regiment who has been wounded while lying in hospital. This instance shows what a place this is. You are under fire in hospital!

I had a most frightfully busy morning and find that work is the only antidote to drive away the dull care that besets one on this narrow neck of land. Except for breakfast I was pretty well busy from 3am in the morning until lunchtime. There is no doubt about it that a squadron leader's job is best under the circumstances. Went on duty in the trenches at the evening stand to and had rather an interesting night. The Colonel ordered us to interrupt the Turks who always dig after dark near Post 17 at our left. Flint laid his machine gun in that direction. Eversden, always ready for fun, took charge of the bomb catapult. At a signal from the Colonel I let off a couple of flares from a Very pistol. It was rather a frost however as no Turks could be seen, but the centre of interest soon shifted as I received a message from Post 15 that they had seen and heard a man crawling about on the *parados* of the trench. I got the men up from their post on to the *parados* and we searched the scrub on the top, at the peril of our lives as there was a tremendous lot of firing going on and bullets were purring through the air. We found nothing but when afterwards I returned to the trench my men told me that they had heard someone jump from the *parados* across the trench to the *parados* higher up. I went along and found that a lot of earth had been dislodged and every sign that what they had reported was true. If one of the enemy had done this he must have got on to a part of the trench between Posts 16 and 17 and he could not escape from there without jumping the trench again. I went down to the Colonel to ask him what was to be done, but he said it must be all nonsense. I was not satisfied and had the trench patrolled. Nothing was seen and in the morning one of my own men confessed to me that it was he who had jumped down into the trench after searching the bushes and dislodged the earth in doing so! I felt rather a fool, but the first part of the mystery remained unsolved – there was undoubtedly a Turk crawling about in the bushes. That same night the Australians tried to take a Turkish listening post not far in front of our trenches. I never saw such a fuss what with bombs, flares and rifle fire. The marvel is that there are so few casualties on these sorts of occasions. I went up to see Eversden fire the bomb catapult again. These bomb catapults are not popular with the men on post duty close-by as they generally get a dose of Turkish shrapnel as a reprisal for letting the thing off!

Wednesday, 10th November
We were relieved by the Bedfords this morning (made Clutterbuck's acquaintance) and we returned to the rest gully. There I found Jack Agnew who tells me Kitchener is supposed to be at Mudros. The news from the Balkans is rather bad. Serbia seems to have thrown up the sponge and complains that an expeditionary force cannot now do her much good. Then what is to happen here is difficult to estimate, and it is certainly depressing to contemplate.

There are rows going on between our squadrons now. It is extraordinary how some men carry strife about with them wherever they go and, under such circumstances, when nerves are rather on edge, these sort of men come very much to the fore. Alas that it should be so here! Surely we have got our hands full enough fighting the Turks, Germans, Austrians, Bulgarians and dysentery without fighting one another?

Thursday, 11th November
An idle day in the rest camp. Felt unwell in the afternoon and had a bad night of it. Was inoculated against cholera.

Friday, 12th November
Feel a bit better in the morning although not well. Lie in my dug-out most of the day. In the evening while we were at mess, an orderly rushes in and announces that if we hear four blasts on the whistle it means that poisoned gas is approaching. Pleasant! Am better this evening.

Saturday, 13th November
Quite well in body again but not so in spirit – feel very depressed at our situation. Kitchener came to the Dardanelles today. He landed at Anzac and proceeded to the trenches of the 1st Australian Division and then apparently left. He didn't come near us. I don't think GHQ likes our pitch and I'm not surprised. I never see any of them here.

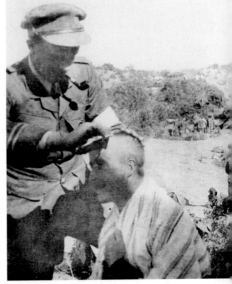

We have had a case of enteric which is serious. Hope it doesn't break out. The dysentery decimates us quite enough without that, and we are getting terribly short of NCOs and men.

I have heard recently of Turks giving themselves up. They always say the same thing when interrogated – that they have got no food and that most of them have lost heart. I don't believe a word of it now the Bulgarians have joined in.

Attempts at normal life – General Horne having his hair cut

Sunday, 14th November
Attended Holy Communion which was held at the end of our gully. The Brigadier was there, a certain number of officers, but very few men. I cannot shake off my depression. This is a most soul-destroying existence – it is wrong I know to be so depressed, but oh! For some good news. I suppose we must bear up and believe all is for the best. The weather is not so promising.

I went over to Stafford Gully in the afternoon to take over from the 11th Londons, but heard to my delight when I returned to camp, that I was to be attached to B Squadron again, so I shall be once more in 'King's Own Avenue', not in command this time, as Frank Goldsmith has returned, but second-in-command. They are short of officers.

Monday, 15th November
My birthday! Not a very pleasant spot to spend it in or a very pleasant way of celebrating it! I am 35 years of age. If there is one benefit which a life such as this confers it is that you resolve if ever you get back to civilization hale and well, and if ever the world comes to its senses again, you will waste less time and, in fact, turn over a new leaf – to use a hackneyed phrase!

All quiet in the trenches until 5 o'clock in the evening when, just as we were having our evening meal near the ridge of the gully, a most tremendous strafe began. We had been warned that some of our troops were going to make an attack on Hill 60. So we eat to the accompaniment of a deafening din. The enemy kept firing shells just over our heads and our guns did ditto in return. I never heard such a noise. However, it did not take away our appetites which are always acute here.

Great huge banks of cumulus cloud were rolling up all the evening. I went on duty in the trenches just after the evening stand to. Soon after I got into them there commenced one of the worst thunderstorms I have ever seen. Mercifully there was not much rain. The soil here cakes so frightfully in wet weather. I heard the attack on Hill 60 was a failure.

Tuesday, 16th November
A very good night's rest. Frank Goldsmith receives some *Fortnum & Mason* boxes by dint of telling them to send him one per day. If you do this you get about two per month! At last we shall be flush of food. This afternoon while sitting in my dug-out a shell burst very violently not far from me. It seemed to rend the whole air and almost raise one off the ground. A German aeroplane flew over our dump. As usual shrapnel was sent up after it. A piece of it fell down into our valley and killed Walter Guinness's servant, a man called Day, tearing his head and shoulder open. He was buried in the valley. I was much grieved – he was a good fellow and used to do a great deal for us at Woodbridge where he was Walter G's chauffer. He was engaged to be married, poor fellow.

Wednesday, 17th November
Two shifts in the trenches last night, which is rather too much of a good thing. Find our mess dug-out wrecked on returning – it looks as if a shell had hit it, but only one shell came over last night and that went far into the next gully. It must have been a landslide.

Oh! The trouble it is to keep clean here. A tremendous sou'west gale sprang up this afternoon, the first real bad weather we have had and it was extraordinarily unpleasant. When it grew dark it began to rain – at 8.30pm. I was sitting in my dug-out while the rain was pattering down on my waterproof sheet and the lightning was playing about in the valleys below, when I noticed a blue flare go up into the sky. The blue flare is a signal to warn of an attack. At once a terrific burst of firing came from the whole way down our line. It was much the best I have yet heard – it was tremendous. The rain was torrential at that moment. I got out of my dug-out and made for the trenches, at first thinking here was the Turkish attack at last. But on second thoughts it struck me that no enemy could easily scale the slopes when they were as slippery as they were this night. It was as much as I could do to get up the short, greasy slope to my trenches. The soil was like butter. At the time of the alarm I was just putting on my trench boots and so great was my haste that I afterwards discovered myself with a trench boot on one leg and a putty on the other! The sight and sound in the trenches was quite awe-inspiring and also rather exhilarating.

Feasting on Fortnam and Mason – General Horne, Flint and 'Apples'

Flares were going up in every direction turning night into day. Everyone was standing to in the rain and firing for all he was worth. In answer to my questions as to if there was anything to fire at, the invariable answer was no, so Frank Goldsmith called a halt to all this din. The rain then ceased and although the wind still blew all was comparative calm again. I had felt some anxiety as this demonstration was going on as Eversden was out at the time with a patrol of about 15 men in no man's land, and with all that firing going on I feared for their lives. It turned out afterwards that they did have a narrow escape. About an hour after the ceasefire, one of Eversden's patrols came in through the tunnel, perspiring and in a great state of mind and asked for me. He said that they were all well but that they had had to lie down flat while the firing was going on as it was all round them. He said Eversden wanted me to give 20 rounds on the machine gun as a signal that it was safe for them to return. This I did and they eventually returned looking like drowned rats. I got them all some brandy, which I kept with me for emergencies. After four hours night duty in the trenches I returned to my dug-out at midnight and found bedding, coat and everything else wet and muddy; part of the structure of my dug-out had collapsed. I had a miserable night of it as it turned bitterly cold towards morning and I had hardly anything dry to sleep in. I had about two hours sleep tonight and two hours last night – it is wonderful how little sleep one can exist on if put to it – but I don't suppose it helps much physically.

Thursday, 18th November
Very cold this morning. The trenches seem to have suffered a bit from last night's rain. It is very fine now and both the sea and islands are a glorious colour. Three more officers are sick this morning. What a weak lot we seem! Few of us seem to be able to stand this sort of life, either officers or men. There seems to be a good deal more shelling than there used to be. German ammunition coming through I suppose.

Bedford Gully

Friday, 19th November

Was on duty in the trenches from 12pm last night until 4am this morning. Beautiful moonlight, but oh! The boringness of that four-hour vigil! However, it might be much worse. Lovely morning again and warmer. The Turks shell our positions pretty well all through the morning and part of the afternoon. Pryor tells me he picked up a bit of shell yesterday with German characters on it. I had a bit of shrapnel shell very near me in my dug-out this morning. Went on duty early in the evening. My men on Post 13 drew my attention to what they thought were Turks working on something on the skyline about 50 yards from us. I told them not to fire as it might be our own men. At that moment the Colonel came up and I pointed the figures out to him. He said he thought they must be our own men but they seemed to me to be too far off for that. After a lot of hesitation he said the men had better fire in that direction. Not being satisfied I gave the order to fire well over the heads of the supposed enemy. Lucky I did so as it turned out to be a working party from the next post, who certainly ought to have given us warning that they were going to get out of the trench.

Saturday, 20th November

This morning we left the trenches for the rest gully. I spent part of the day trying to find a place where our men could practice bombing. It struck me as rather an absurd predicament that here, actually in active service, we should still be learning how to fight – that is the worst of an improvised army. There seems to be no place to practice which is not under fire – so restricted is our area. Had tea at the Brigadier's mess this evening at the bottom of the gully – they do themselves very well here and have got the most comfortable dug-outs. They are too good to be called dug-outs. They resemble log cabins with this difference; that the logs are sandbags. However, I should have thought that they are very much alike under shell-fire.

Walter Guinness has taken over temporary command of the 10th London Regiment.

Sunday, 21st November

Everything seems wrong. Bad news follows bad news. All our best men seem to have gone sick and are away off the peninsula – lucky men! I have been reading Asquith's speech on the Dardanelles in the newspapers in which he throws up the sponge and says the whole thing is a failure. He takes the trouble to exonerate Winston Churchill, who is of course, chiefly to blame. Bitter cold weather has set in which sends me to my dug-out at night in despair.

Monday, 22nd November

Am cheered by the arrival of two parcels from Alec and Theo this morning. Oh! The joy of receiving parcels. Living under these vile conditions the mind becomes the mind partly of an animal and partly of a child. Oh! To be back in civilization again! Hear a report that Greece is in against us. If this is true it will be too much to bear. Took a bombing class this evening. No accident occurred and although particularly in view of the enemy, we were not shelled or interrupted in any way.

Tuesday, 23rd November

Jack Agnew came into the gully this morning and told me that my name had been sent into Headquarters for the post of brigade bombing officer. I do not quite know what this entails but a change of occupation might be a change for good. Second-in-command of a squadron is a do-nothing job – and anything to get away from Stafford Gully. Our chaplain had to leave us today with a bad attack of malaria. Everyone is leaving – all the best fellows – for one cause or another, that is one of the many disheartening features of this campaign, and we have no resources or reinforcements to take their place. Consequently, it is impossible to organise a unit for any definite purpose. Another bombing class this afternoon, but a hopeless failure as all the fuses are bad.

Wednesday, 24th November

A do-nothing day, varied by two exciting personal experiences. In the afternoon I went down to Brigade Headquarters to examine some bombs which the engineers had sent up. While I was doing so a shrapnel shell burst up above me and a piece came within a few inches of my shoulder. I walked away and found the Brigadier a few yards further on examining a jagged piece of shell which had just fallen at his feet. I went further up into the rest camp and while walking up the gully, the Turk started shelling and I received a shower of shrapnel, apparently straight at me, but not a piece touched me. I jumped into the nearest dug-out where I found Geoffrey Barker taking shelter.

Thursday, 25th November
Wake up early with something on my mind. I remembered that we had left a lot of live bombs that we had thrown out into the open at bomb practice yesterday and which had not exploded. It was impossible to collect them in the daytime as that spot was in full view of the enemy. I had meant to have them collected after dark, but somehow the matter was not attended to and now it made me uneasy to have left a number of high explosive bombs lying about on the ground which was often shelled by the enemy, and which was quite close to where some of our brigade lived. So I arose in the dark at about 5 o'clock. There was a good deal of enemy sniping going on and when I reached the open space where the bombs were it looked much lighter than I cared for and I admit that I decided to give up my quest. But when I got back to my dug-out I felt so ashamed of myself that I returned and collected no less than ten errant bombs. It was daylight by then and I did not take long over the job – it was a nasty spot. Early in the morning we marched down to our trenches in Stafford Gully. I really thought I had said goodbye to that beastly place, but not a bit of it. It is more beastly than ever, a real rat-trap with no possible means of exercise.

This diary must seem a catalogue of grievances, disappointments and bad news, but all these are to be had in plenty here. The worst news we have had yet arrived in the shape of a gloomy War Office telegram soon after breakfast. The Bulgarians seem to be victorious and our own military situation grave. In the evening came another piece of intelligence which made us all feel uneasy. Looked like rain before dinner, and if it rains in Stafford Gully it will be Hades at once. Luckily it turned fine later though bitterly cold. At about 12 o'clock at night I heard that Walter Guinness had been out on a patrol and that one of his men had been badly wounded. I saw him being carried in on a stretcher. I had a disturbed night.

Friday, 26th November
Three shells burst over our trenches this morning quite close to me while I was on duty. It is a most disgusting sensation. If anybody says he likes being under fire the truth is not in him. The rest of the day was quiet. In the afternoon the Colonel comes up and tells us that the whole of the East Anglian Division (except ourselves) are being moved off the peninsula. I go up with him to see Walter Guinness, who now commands two of the regiments of that division. Walter seems quite annoyed at having to leave and go to Mudros. He said to me with scorn 'Fancy Mudros!' – I confess that Mudros would seem like paradise to me. I envied these fellows going away.

Just before the evening stand to a violent wind began to blow and storm clouds drifted up over our heads. Then there burst upon us a terrible thunderstorm with a perfect deluge of rain which lasted four or five hours. Unfortunately I was on duty in

A typical view of Anzac

The surrounding countryside

the trenches directly after the stand to and I had not even got a fleece coat on. This I left behind in my dug-out which, on my return, I found to be flooded. I never saw such a night. After I had come out of the trenches I went into the gully and had an improvised meal of sardines and cheese. While there I heard a roaring sound in the distance getting nearer and louder every moment and then all of a sudden the gully was converted into a rushing, raging torrent which carried Dixies, haversacks and every sort of thing down with it – a regular flood. Tomkin, fearing an attack, ordered us all into the trenches and for the rest of the night we had to wade about knee-deep in water, perishingly cold, altogether a vile experience. At about three in the morning I met Limmington who told me we had received orders to return to the rest gully and that some New Zealand regiments were going to take our place.

Saturday, 27th November

It came on again to rain in the morning. The New Zealanders turned up very late and we had to wait about a long time in mud and misery. They did look so despondent when they saw the condition of our trenches. I must say they did not look comfortable.

When we returned to Bedford Gully I met Birkbeck of the Norfolks who told me that we were going to share Hill 60 with the Norfolk Yeomanry – Hill 60 has an evil reputation – and that we are to construct a new rest camp – awful fun after we had just spent six weeks in perfecting one here! – Hill 60 is notorious as being one of the worst, or the worst pitch in the peninsula. I am told, however, we have not got the worst bit of it. Anyway, I am not sorry to leave Stafford Gully of evil memory.

A good deal of shell-fire of all kinds going on this morning. I am feeling frightfully depressed. I cannot feel that anything that I am doing here is of the slightest use to anybody. This was not at all my pre-conceived notion of war.

Our ships today are making a tremendous demonstration. I suppose to counteract the bad news from the Balkans which continues to make us more melancholy every

78

day. In the evening while we were at mess, the Colonel comes round and says that I am to go off to Imbros tomorrow with several other officers representing the 54th Division, to arrange about a rest camp.

I was overjoyed at the idea of having a few days away from here. I felt how delightful it would be to take some violent exercise all over the island free from shot and shell.

Sunday, 28th November

Had a grievous disappointment. When I looked out from my dug-out in the early morning I thought the atmosphere looked rather odd and a further investigation revealed the fact that the ground was covered with snow! My heart once again sank within me. Later I received a message that no boats could go to Imbros. I could have cried with disappointment. I was so looking forward to that brief holiday and change of occupation. In the afternoon came the news that my squadron has got to start off at 3 o'clock tomorrow morning to relieve the Norfolk Yeomanry in their line of trenches, which is one of the worst in the peninsula. Tomkin today went up to have a look at them and came down again with the gloomiest accounts. This is not a pleasant prospect for us. All my blankets and coats are still damp from the night before last. The weather has not been fine enough to dry them. Now as I write I am in my dug-out wrapped in them. The wind is howling and it is snowing hard. How I love my dug-out now and how loath I am to leave it! We are suffering the hardships of Arctic explorers now, in addition to everything else. Well, we must grin and bear it. Our water has been limited to three pints per man, per day. We cannot even carry our packs up to the trenches tomorrow!

Monday, 29th November

I shall never forget this day as long as I live. One of the worst I have ever spent. After hardly any sleep I get up at 3am. It is dark. The wind is still howling. It is freezing hard. Snow covers the ground. Luckily there is a moon. I come out of my dug-out and I look on a most depressing scene. The men gradually collect after a great deal of swearing on the part of the officers. Obviously the heart is out of them, and out there in the snow and dark and cold I feel our situation to be not unlike that of Napoleon's army in Russia. We somehow get the men lined up. One falls down in a faint at my feet, weak with illness and cold and despair. At about 4 o'clock we start off up along a sap above the Welsh Horse camp and over two ridges. At one point we were blocked by Ghurkhas coming the other way. Poor little devils. They were absolutely frozen and I saw one leaning up against the wall of the sap sobbing like a child. In places the sap was knee-deep in half-frozen slush. I shall never forget that awful march – it seemed interminable. It was a nightmare. At last we arrived at Hill 60 and certainly nothing that I had heard about its horrors were exaggerated. The trenches vary from 30 to 70 yards from the Turkish positions on the top of a low ridge. Bodies are buried in the parapet. There was a hand protruding in one place. This looks very grim by moonlight. When the Welsh Horse were digging in this trench a few days ago I understand they had to hack through a wall of Turkish dead!

We post our sentinels and retire to our dump immediately behind the firing line. We have got nothing whatsoever to eat. Day dawns and it becomes fine though bitterly cold. At one point, where our trenches dip down into a valley, they are flooded. If this gets much worse we will be isolated from our communications. The Welsh Horse have however made an indifferent job of stopping it up at the back. I doubt it will be of any use. This fact does not seem to have struck the authorities. Nothing strikes them. They don't come up here to see how awful things are. If bad weather came these trenches would be quite untenable with the handful of men we are at present. We are terribly short-handed.

Thanks to the mismanagement of the A Squadron mess I had nothing to eat on this awful day – a day which began at 3am. At sundown I went to see Frank Goldsmith and he gave me a nip of brandy. This is not the sort of life to lead on an empty stomach. However, we are not the only ones that are miserable. My men tell me they can hear the Turks sobbing in their trenches. I felt queer in the evening; my blankets and coats had never dried. My dug-out, which adjoins the trenches at the back, is not a bad one but the noise of firing, the perpetual plunk plunk of the bullets in the parapet and the bombing, which goes on so close, is depressing. At night I went on duty from 9.30pm to midnight. It was alarming to realise how weakly we held this trench. Turks could come in. All went well. Near 12 o'clock the Welsh Horse were making an enormous tunnel under the enemy trenches in order to mine them, a fine piece of work. I went down it and could hear the enemy countermining. Close to this was one of our posts, and I suddenly received a message that one of my men had been shot in the face there. I told the others to place him at the mouth of the tunnel as this post was so close to the enemy I did not want them to show any lights there. I went off to get the stretcher bearers. By the time the stretcher bearers arrived the man was dead. At midnight I went off duty but I did not get much sleep. So ended a bad day.

Sunday, 30th November
When I woke this morning I heard some commotion going on. I turned out and walked along the sap to Tomkin's dug-out. There was an open space in front of it. Tomkin called out to me to run across it into the trench as there was a Turkish sniper somewhere at the back who had killed one of our men close-by. I ran into the trench and found the poor man's body at the bottom of the trench. His brother, who was also in the squadron, was standing by him leaning against the trench and sobbing. I tried to say some words of comfort to him. It is such scenes as these which make one hate this war. I found out that Tomkin had behaved very gallantly. This poor man was one of the stretcher bearers that I had called last night. At the time of his being killed he was laying out the body of the sentry who had been shot in the night. He was doing this at the back of the trench, just below Tomkin's dug-out, when he was shot in the back. Tomkin rushed down and hauled him up into the trench. If it was a Turkish sniper, he must have crawled round to the back of our positions, but as he did not fire again the bullet may have been one of those ubiquitous overs from anywhere, which added so much to the unpleasantries of life on the peninsula. Whatever it was, Tomkin showed great pluck in what he did.

Men at work in the gully

During the cold weather one of our men was slightly wounded. He went down to the beach hospital where there was such a crowd he became frostbitten and had to have his foot amputated.

This morning I felt so collapsed I decided to report sick. Accordingly I retired down the sap to the next valley where I found the doctor who sent me to the EMB field hospital. I found Coombes there, a very nice doctor who had come out with us on the *Olympic*. He gave me his dug-out and it was such a relief to get dry and warm again. I had been living and sleeping in damp things in this awful cold atmosphere for three or four days. I went to bed at once and was very thankful for a real rest in dry clothing.

Wednesday, 1st December
Did not sleep very much last night but woke up feeling very much more comfortable. Spent the day in bed thankful for a short rest. Doctors congregate in the dug-out in the evening and discuss the general situation and how we shall fare in the winter. If this is to be judged by the standard of the last few days we shall fare very badly. Dawson of the ASC came in with gloomy news.

There is actually a fire in this dug-out but it smokes too dreadfully. Had a whole batch of letters from home with the usual notice of parcels coming, which hardly ever arrive.

Thursday, 2nd December
Again did not sleep very much but I got out of bed and went to see Jack Agnew who is also sick and very gloomy. A lovely morning, although it froze very hard last night, the snow seems to have gone. The doctor showed me round the hospital, which consists of one or two marquee tents. It is quite small, really only a dressing station. He showed me a hole in the canvas of the operating tent through which a bullet came last Saturday

and killed one of their orderlies. The doctor asked me whether I wanted to be sent down to the beach hospital, which meant evacuation, or whether I wanted to return to my regiment. I wanted to return to my regiment. After lunch I set off back to Bedford Gully. The saps were very muddy in places. How they get the transport along in this weather passes my understanding. When I arrived I found the gully in possession of the Norfolk Yeomanry; our regiment being up at Hill 60. I occupied Grissell's dug-out which was moderately comfortable. Grissell had a curious experience in this dug-out a short while since. It was at night – his hand was grazed by a bullet while he was resting in his shelter. Later that day he happened to open his cigarette case and found the bullet inside it! I was lucky not to be hit too as the firing was tremendous at night and the overs were cracking overhead all night long. A great deal of shelling going on – all the noise seemed to come from the direction of Hill 60.

Friday, 3rd December
Eversden has rolled up here and is sharing my dug-out. He has been sick too. He is a remarkable young fellow. He joined us from the second line, where he had got into trouble owing to some love affair just as we were starting for the Dardanelles. He is one of the few I have met who enjoyed the war. He is fearless to a fault. I cannot help liking him despite his many shortcomings. I should say that he was a good fellow at heart but badly brought up – would probably reform under good influence. But as a soldier he is a tiger. Excellent at night patrol, he is generally employed for the nasty jobs. He insists on reading me a long screed he has written for the *Anzac Magazine*. Terrible stuff! He is the most ingenious fellow as a mechanic or draftsman but no good as a writer. Poor Eversden! There is something very attractive about him in spite of his faults!

Disappointing weather again – a grey day, mist and some wind. Feel very low still. Get through some writing; spend most of the day in the Colonel's quarters. Retire to roost early. Terrific firing going on in the direction of our trenches which lasts for about a quarter of an hour.

Saturday, 4th December
Still feel low and weak but am going to return to duty. The squadron turn up with tremendous stories of mining and countermining in our trenches last night which caused the above mentioned outburst of fire.

At a quarter to four I set off in command of what is left of A Squadron (38 men) to a valley just behind Hill 60, to be in support of the Norfolk Yeomanry, who are in the trenches and holding them very lightly. Arrive there and report myself to Colonel Morse, a colonel of the Norfolk Yeomanry, and receive my instructions. He says, in the event of two blue flares going up, I am to advance with my squadron in extended order over the ridge which divides us from Hill 60 and reinforce in the trenches. As the enemy are continuously raking this ridge with rifle fire there probably would not be much left of us if we made the attempt – but this scheme was probably concocted by someone who does not care very much what happens. As I was talking to Colonel Morse (I was

Our dug-outs

standing outside his dug-out and he was inside) I saw two blue flares go up in the sky. I reported this to him and he put his head out as the fireworks were subsiding. I watched him anxiously making up his mind what to do. He was a calm old boy (luckily it wasn't our colonel) and he said to me – 'Well, I should wait a moment.' I did and it was of great relief to me to see spurt up into the air a regular Brocks, bereft of blue flares. We then made up our minds that this could not be our signal. We found out afterwards that the Ghurkhas had got the wind up and thought they had better turn night into day. I make arrangements now to spend the night with Limmington in an extemporised cook-house. Two Welsh Horse officers turn up and claim it as their very own but very kindly let me remain and doss down with them. Saw some stretcher bearers bringing along the body of a Norfolk Yeoman who had been killed by shrapnel in our trenches today. This is a very noisy valley as all the overs rattle down here.

Sunday, 5th December
Return with the squadron to camp. Report to the Colonel and emphasize the fact that I only had 38 men with me. He said it was nonsense, that I had 98 and produced all sorts of lists of fellows who were down in hospital. We have several new hardships to bear. There has been no bread or fresh meat for a week. There have been no mails for a fortnight (whenever it blows, the pier is broken and the lighters cannot land anything on Anzac Beach). Nearly all the news we hear is very serious indeed. The 54th East Anglian Division, to which we have up to now been attached, has now left the peninsula. German guns and artillery are, we hear, getting through.

Our efforts to keep the Sabbath here are somewhat hampered. Our *padre* has gone away sick – and when I tried to read the pocket Bible I always carry about with me, batmen crowded round my dug-out and employed themselves at laundry work. An enormous quantity of shells has been sent over by the enemy, more than I had ever known before. One of our men has been killed in the gully and three or four others wounded in consequence. Branwell Jackson has been given a staff appointment on the GOC's staff at Anzac. He went down to dine with his new chief tonight and he came back with the first really good bit of news I have heard since we arrived here – General Godley had been told that the Russians had broken through into Bulgaria. If things go well in that quarter it should make a difference here. But I do not believe any news implicitly which is not in print.

Monday, 6th December
A mail in, which is always a great joy, but there were very few letters for me. Spent a more pleasant day than usual. The sun at last comes out and still better, Flint lends me a book. The delight of reading again was beyond words. At night I have to light my extemporised lamp (Eversden taught me how to make one) which fumed and stank furiously but the temptation to read overmastered the discomfort.

Our numbers are now so attenuated that three squadrons are to be formed into two, but it means that we officers will have less rest as far as I can make out. Another mail in today and plenty of letters. Hear that the Norfolk regimental Sergeant Major was killed in one of our trenches last night.

Tuesday, 7th December
Another morning in Bedford Gully. Cannot find out what the news is with regard to Russia – they never seem to let us have any news here. In the afternoon I am suddenly ordered to take the squadron over to the valley behind Hill 60 to be in support of the Norfolk Yeomanry. I fancy the authorities are getting the wind up about Hill 60. I am not surprised.

Soon after we arrived at our destination they carried down the body of the Norfolk Yeomanry regimental Sergeant Major who was killed recently.

In the evening I disposed my men in dug-outs and then retired to rest myself – but not for long. The Adjutant of the Norfolk Yeomanry, Ruggles-Brise, came to tell me there was a message in to the effect that the Turks had removed their wire from in front of their trenches at Sud el Bahr which looked as if they meant to attack, and that we must be on the alert. However Sud el Bahr was not particularly close to us, but an hour or two later just as I was dozing off to sleep I heard the Adjutant's steps coming towards me again with a message to say that there was a report that the Turks were removing their wire on Hill 60. This looked like business for us. Colonel Morse told me that I was not to do anything but merely to have my men ready and to stand them to early in the morning. It was rather a jumpy night but nothing desperate happened after all. Earlier in the day I witnessed a wonderful bombardment by our fleet, the shells bursting in the direction of Salt Lake. I don't believe these naval shells do the enemy any harm, but they look and sound as if they were blowing up the whole peninsula.

Wednesday, 8th December

As a consequence of last night's message we had to stand to at five o'clock this morning. The rest of the day was certainly rather peaceful. Great changes have now taken place in our regiment. We have been here over two months and the wastage during that time, which under any circumstance would have been considerable, is all the greater in my regiment as our draft from the second line, which joined us just before we started from England, was such a miserable soft lot. They all go sick at once. We have amalgamated our three squadrons into two. The effect of this upon my own career is that A Squadron ceases to exist and I go to D Squadron under Pryor, of whom I am awfully fond. He is a good chap and cheerful. I went back to Bedford Gully. The regiment moved out of it to take up its new quarters further east, but I stayed behind with D Squadron. To my delight I was able to buy a dozen candles off the squadron Sergeant Major today who had had a supply up from the beach. I also borrowed a book from Pryor and the combination of candles and book, when I turned into my dug-out at night, was a luxury I felt I hardly deserved, so great did it seem. No-one knows how great are these small deprivations. Going without candles, water, books, underclothing, papers etc. for months on end has an accumulative affect on one's spirits.

Thursday, 9th December

A very peaceful day in Bedford Gully with nothing to do. Went over to see the Norfolk Yeomanry in our new quarters and had a talk with FFolkes, the new chaplain who seems optimistic about the Balkan situation and our own. A sad episode happened a short time ago. FFolkes was burying a man in the Welsh Horse when one of his comrades, who was standing by the grave, fell dead from a stray bullet.

These new quarters have a much wider view and there are some olive groves in the valley. Shells were bursting quite close to us, but we seem fairly under cover. The men still laugh when they come along. My own nerves rather on edge.

Friday, 10th December

I spend the morning digging in our new quarters – dreadful sort of work but useful. Am getting a curious sort of affection of the skin on my fingers which look as if they are rotting. Probably comes from digging in poisonous ground. We get another post – a great blessing. The afternoon I spend in washing and laundry work with what little water that there is. Not at all an unpleasant day as days go here, but I feel I cannot stand the peninsula much longer.

Saturday, 11th December

Another morning's digging and another afternoon's slacking. Rumours good and bad floating about – mostly bad. It is a blessing being in Bedford Gully with hardly anyone here. Officers number six; Tomkin, Wodehouse, Barker, Pryor, Crisp and self, about the best selection in the Yeomanry. Call on Hugh Buxton who is ADC at Divisional Headquarters. They are comfortable there, although they have been badly shelled. I had a most excellent tea with them – cake – which is a wonderful rarity. I long for it at all hours of the day.

In our quarters we are very short of water and it was a great blessing to drink tea almost *ad lib*. Sometimes in my squadron we have to make up our minds whether we will have a cup of tea or a shave, so short is the water.

Jack Agnew has now left the peninsula sick. It is extraordinary how few of the old lot are now left. We ought to have an extra medal and bonus, those of us who are still here! Walked back with Geoffrey Barker in the evening by the Achil Dere. Oh! For a good strapping walk over the hills. If we walk over the hills here we are machine-gunned. I do long for something intelligent to do. Hanging about under fire is awful. Feel hopelessly depressed in the evening. We ought not to complain as much as we do, but it is the lack of sensible and appropriate work that is so overpowering.

Sunday, 12th December
Another quiet day. We started trying to dig officers' dug-outs in our new quarters but it is not a good place for them.

Monday, 13th December
The New Zealanders threaten to come and take possession of Bedford Gully this morning. Walk over to our new quarters in the morning and I hear the first piece of hopeful intelligence I have heard for two months. It is to the effect that the Norfolk Yeomanry have orders to leave – and I am left wondering if this is too much to hope that we shall have received the same orders. For the present the Colonel is not here, so I must possess my soul in patience until I know if the news applies to the whole brigade – any relief would be intense. What we all want is a rest to our nerves which have been strained for two months without intermission. If we could only be away from the sound of shot and shell for a day or two we should all feel different men. Hear rumours and one piece of news for certain. We are to send on an advanced party some time or other. We are to go into the trenches

Rest camp

in the usual way tomorrow. I share a dug-out with John Wodehouse.

I met the Colonel who looked very grave indeed and he said we must not talk about our move. He also gave us certain orders which convinced me it was something more than just a move of the Eastern Mounted Brigade to Imbros for a rest. There had been a whisper of general evacuation in the air before this and when I went back to Bedford Gully for lunch Geoffrey Barker met me with the intelligence that he had obtained in the morning from an RE officer to the effect that the Government had decided to evacuate the peninsula, and that it had been going on already for two or three days and was expected to be complete by Thursday. It struck me as being marvellous that this RE officer (who I believe was a staff officer) should have given away this information to someone he did not know.

This news was a blow indeed, and difficult to take in. What this means for the Empire no-one can tell. It is one of the greatest blows conceivable to our prestige. Went into the trenches this evening on Hill 60. While there, the Turks started exploding them with some nasty high explosives. The shells went rather over our heads and landed among the Welsh Horse – killing one of them and wounding three others. Returned to Bedford Gully and destroyed all the army papers that I have got which would be of any use to the enemy as the chances of being taken prisoner have considerably increased.

Tuesday, 14th December
We make an early start for the trenches and stumble along in the dark towards Hill 60 feeling dejected to the last degree. The Colonel meets me at the support gully and tells me he wants me to leave today with the advanced party. I am not at all loath to go but it is dreadful to feel that some of the regiment are staying behind. This idea is, I am told, to gradually get every regiment away by driblets. Since the evacuation began they have moved about 2,000 away each night from the three bays so far. Most of the guns have gone. That is painfully apparent I should have thought, even to the enemy. Another circumstance that must be apparent to the enemy is that all the hospital tents have been removed and also, if they were half-sharp they would notice that hardly any smoke is going up from the incinerators in the various gullies – as a rule there is a perfect fog of it every evening. I thought the whole place looked horribly deserted the last time I walked over from Bedford Gully to our new quarters.

When we reached the trenches we were told a Turkish deserter gave himself up last night and imparted the information that 60,000 Turks had returned to Constantinople, sick of the whole show. I never think the word of a deserter is much worth taking but what I did notice today was that there seemed to be hardly any Turks in their trenches at Hill 60. The sentries say that when they fire at the enemy a cloud of birds fly up from the trenches, which looks as if they are unoccupied.

Nevertheless, they seem to be mining all round us and the Welsh Horse miners report the Turk is digging a mine just near ours. We did not get very much of a shelling today, in fact everything seemed pretty quiet and one does not quite know what to make of it all. In the evening I get orders to report myself at Regimental

Our trenches

Headquarters whither I accordingly bend my steps, thankful to shake the dust of the trenches off my feet, but deeply anxious as to the fate of those who are left behind. I pick up about 30 men and together with Welsh Horse and Norfolk Yeomanry details we march to the Brigade Headquarters. I find Hugh Buxton there who says we are to keep in close together. It was now pitch dark and off we went for the last time down the Achil Dere. It was with very different feelings than those we had the first time we climbed up it on our arrival here. It was difficult to analyse my feelings on this, my last night on the peninsula. Many things were troubling me. I was extremely exhausted, and had agonising pains in my legs. I am sure I could not have held out for another day in this place. It was with a heavy heart, although with a sense of relief, that I was leaving. We rested once or twice on the way down. On one of these waits one of my men got a bullet clean through the wooden part of his rifle. It would have been a bad business if he had been killed just as he was departing. We passed a great many Indian contingents and they nearly all made a deprecating gesture with their hands with smiling exclamation '*fee-nished*', and it struck me then most forcibly what an evil effect the evacuation may produce in India. There was a good deal of rifle and machine gun fire going on upon the cliffs above us as we descended to the beach. But mercifully we had no casualties at all. When we arrived down by the sea they kept us waiting in the sap as the enemy was shelling the lighters. I was suffering in my limbs and had to alternately stand and sit while we waited until each position became unbearable. They moved us on a few hundred yards at intervals until at last we reached the mouth of the sap, which was not far from the little pier. It was a fine night although beginning to blow. Above us rose those famous Anzac cliffs which the Australians scaled in their original landing. All around us were the remains of the great beach dump, now nothing but a wreck with hardly any lights showing. I could see the shrapnel bursting in the air over the sea. During one of our interminable waits I left my men in the sap and went out to explore. I never saw such a sight. It was quite clear that evacuation had been going on for some days. I went up to see the parcel post office. All the officials had left and the whole place had been looted and ransacked. There was a huge camp hospital all deserted. Most of the official dug-outs on the beach were now unattended. I never saw such a depressing spectacle as the whole dump presented. On my return a man met me with a parcel on the road and asked me if I was Captain Cadogan. How he knew it was I, I have never discerned!

At last at about 10.30pm we received orders to bundle on to the lighter as quickly as possible. This we did without mishap, although the Military Landing Officer seemed to be losing his head badly. I had got some of the Colonel's kit with me and put a man in charge of it who looked after it so well it fell into the sea. After a great deal of fuss and shouting we started out seaward. We could not find our ship. We kept going alongside one ship after another but not one of them was the right one. Then to my horror, after exhausting all the possibilities, we started going back to Anzac pier and as the gale was getting up I had visions of being set down once more on the peninsula and never getting off again! However, the Captain of the lighter was evidently a strong-minded man as he decided to turn round again and ask the nearest ship to take us off. This the Captain of the nearest ship agreed to do. We got a shell very near us as we were executing some of these manoeuvres in the bay, but fortunately it missed us altogether. When the lighter came alongside the ship the sea was so rough it was difficult to board her. The scene of transferring our men from the lighter to the ship, which kept on banging up against each other, was one of indescribable confusion. I confess I heaved a sigh of relief when I got on to that miserable cattleboat. Never did a ship seem such a haven of refuge – having been nearly 60 days continuously under fire, and so I leave the Dardanelles; disappointed, disillusioned and deeply anxious for the fate of those of the regiment who remained. Conscious that I had taken part in a British reverse, not a very pleasant reflection.

We weighed anchor fairly soon after we had all been safely tucked in. I was feeling very unwell and exhausted, and after disposing of my men down below I went to a sort of saloon where there was a horrible red, plush sofa which seemed the height of luxury to me. You could still hear the rattle of musketry on the shore and the boom of the guns. I dozed off and after an hour or so sat up and listened – there was the noise of paddle wheels but the other sound I heard no more.

Wednesday, 15th December
I awoke to find our ship in Mudros Harbour (Isle of Lemnos). We went alongside the Tunisian almost at once and boarded her. She was one of the Allan line. We found her a very comfortable boat indeed with good cabins and good food, but I was too ill to appreciate any of these luxuries, which, under conditions of good health, would have presented such a delightful contrast to the Dardanelles. I shared a cabin with Harry Birkbeck, who was in charge of some Norfolk Yeomanry details. FFolkes, the Norfolk Yeomanry *padre* was on board and a number of RAMC doctors. I collapsed into bed with fever – Harry Birkbeck did the same with jaundice. An army official came on board to tell us we were bound for Egypt. We remained for about four days in harbour. When I got rid of the fever I discovered I had jaundice. I shall never forget the first bath I had on board. I had not had a bath for months and had rarely had my clothes off. Merely for a few seconds *per diem* in sections, washing, or attempting to wash, in an inch or two of cold water in a canvas bag so that I had not had an opportunity of examining myself. I received a shock. I was a skeleton and bright yellow from the jaundice!

Letter to Alec Cadogan

Letter to Alec Cadogan

Editors' notes:

This letter, found with Cadogan's diaries was addressed to his brother Alec. It was written in regulation purple pencil on 'Sultan Hussein Club, Alexandria' notepaper. It was never finished and was not sent.

January 1916

My dear Alec,

I think I last wrote to you a night or two ago from my tent, just before turning-in. That night we had the worst gale that I believe they have had for 30 years, and as I was practically on the sea-shore you can imagine what fun we had in our little tents. A great number were blown flat. I managed to save mine by clinging onto ropes and various other devices, but the storm of sand which accompanied the wind was awful.

I thought I'd write you a letter in my spare time giving you some of my impressions of the peninsula, which I was not able to do at the time I was there. As you know, I am perfectly ignorant of all military matters: I know nothing of strategy and I saw no battle in the open therefore I cannot supply you with any information or offer any opinion – it would be presumption, and I believe, insubordination if I passed any strictures upon any of the official news from the Dardanelles. This does not prevent my having formed my own opinion on the subject but it does prevent me airing these opinions. However, if I should not bore you I'd like to add a postscript to the letters I sent you from there which can, now that we have evacuated the place, no longer be indiscreet or prejudicial to anybody's interest, in the extremely unlikely event of the document getting into enemy hands.

Starting then with the superfluous admission that I know nothing about matters military, I can at least say this in defence of the following comments. One way or another I saw practically the whole of our line at Anzac – occupying in the course of nine weeks a great part of that line and visiting another part that my regiment never did occupy. This means I saw our position from Lone Pine, which was our extreme right at Anzac (and commands a vast view including Achi Baba) to our extreme left at Hill 60, which adjoined and overlooked our positions at Suvla.

Now, one of the first things that struck me forcibly after I landed, was the fact that practically all our main communications from the beach up to the trenches were river-beds. They were dry, of course, at the season of the year that I saw them and some were wide and deep, others narrow and shallow. When I tell you that at Anzac the Turkish lines were nearly all, if not all, on a much higher elevation than ours and that consequently they could overlook, not only our positions, but a great deal of the country inbetween our positions and the sea, you will realise the extreme importance of invisible means of communication. Not only invisible, but protected from shell and machine gun-fire. The main artery which supplied us with ammunition and food from the beach was a river-bed called the Achil Dere, which is marked as a river on maps. At night, mule carts used to bring provisions to us up this dry river-bed and we used it as a means of communication with our rest camp both by day and night. The greater part of it afforded us complete concealment from the gaze of the enemy. As far as I could discover, no alternative had been provided in the event of bad weather which converted these *nullahs* into rivers. To get out of the Achil Dere and walk on the bank or in any of the open country was practically speaking, certain death.

Had we experienced bad weather (which we might easily have done in November and December and certainly would have done in January, February and March) I fail to see how we could have communicated with the beach. The answer that the mule carts could come up in the open at night is no good, because machine guns could be trained in the daytime on all the best targets and fired at night directly the enemy perceived, either by light of the moon or by the noise which a string of supply carts must make, that the mule train was passing the target. We did, as you know, have a few days' bad weather and then the condition of these *nullahs* became almost unbearable. So thought three men in my division who one day, being tired of pounding up to their waists in water and mud, got out on to the bank, and were all three instantly hit by Turkish snipers. From personal experiences I draw the conclusion that if bad weather had lasted for two or three weeks, a large part of our line at Anzac would have been completely cut off from all supplies. One of these experiences was during those awful two or three days of snow when I went up to Hill 60 and was, from three in the morning (which was the time I started up there) until sundown, without food or drink, owing to the hopeless condition of the means of communication. The other experience was during a most terrific thunderstorm in a certain gully, at the bottom of which was one of these dry river-beds. It was actually in this dry river-bed that our dug-outs were situated, hollowed out in the river-bank. It was the only possible place where we could get concealment or protection from enemy fire. The thunderstorm had been raging for about four hours when I heard a roaring sound in the distance which rapidly approached and eventually reached me. It was the sound of running water. In this short space of time our dry river-bed had been converted into a rushing torrent and instead of supplies coming up to us I saw saucepans, haversacks, food etc. floating away down back to the sea! From these slight experiences I drew my own conclusions as to what would happen when the real and enduring bad weather came.

Nobody who has inhabited Anzac could possibly entertain any idea of holding it through the months of February and March.

The next thing that struck me was the lack of a suitable harbour. Anzac is no harbour at all – it is an open roadstead. When the sou'west wind blows, and it seems to blow pretty frequently in the autumn and winter, you can neither embark nor land there and as far as I could see, even when there was only a slight sou'west breeze, this was the case. But, bad job as this was, it was not the worst consequence of the sou'west wind blowing. Whenever it blew a gale from this quarter the pier was smashed up and so were most of the lighters, so that even when the gale had gone down you could not land anything or embark until these were repaired. This was often a matter of days. We used to know this to our cost because on these occasions our mail and our food became more scanty than they were in normal times.

A few words now upon disease. When I was on the peninsula I was not supposed to say anything about it, but now the cat is out the bag, I can. I quite fearlessly express the opinion that if nothing else was going to stop us 'getting through' in the autumn or winter – disease would have done the trick. Take my regiment as an example. Roughly speaking, about three-fifths of it were evacuated from the peninsula owing to disease. The figures regarding the disease among the troops in the Dardanelles were beyond all belief. But perhaps the most remarkable figures were those of the casualties caused by those two or three cold days at Suvla. Suvla was much the greatest sufferer from the cold because the trenches and dug-outs were on a plain instead of (as with us and Helles) on the side of a hill. The consequence was that they were flooded out and had to face the cold with no protection. A moderate estimate of the casualties from cold at Suvla during those two or three days was 8,000. About 200 died. Many of them were found (as the doctor told me) standing dead at their posts. However, now I am digressing. The disease I maintain, would have finished us. Men were going down much faster than the necessary minimum of reinforcements could have replaced them – and prolonged cold would have rendered this state of affairs ten times worse.

Another thing that struck me as rendering the idea of hanging on through the winter impossible was the physical nature of the soil. On the boat which took me to the Dardanelles, the so-called conducting officer told me that he had recently conducted a geological expert from the British Museum to the peninsula. This expert had expressed the view that our trenches and dug-outs would melt in continued wet weather. I am sure he was right. It was a most peculiar kind of clay which looked beautiful: hard and durable in fine weather, but became like soap in the wet. This meant that to make our trenches tenable under bad weather conditions, we should have required a vast army of engineers, which I need hardly tell you we had not got, nor were likely to get.

Then there was the food question, which may seem like a minor trifle but which is more important from the point of view of keeping a regiment in health and consequently up to strength than almost anything else. With no harbour, limited means of transport and countless difficulties of all sorts, it was impossible to feed us properly. That is to say, to prevent us suffering from disorders due directly to either the quality or scarcity of the food. I quite admit that at the risk of being insubordinate I am going, for the first time in this letter, to criticise authority. A perfectly avoidable defect in the Commissariat was the monotony of the supplies. This affected men's health. I believe any doctor will tell you that if you eat the same food day after day it will nauseate you, however little fastidious you may be. It is not a question of being fastidious – or the reverse. It is a physical fact that you cannot eat the same food day after day without it producing sickness of some kind after time. Well then, take for one instance, why was the jam supplied to the troops always apricot? I am obliged to acknowledge that towards the end of our time, authority began to recognise this and to vary it. This was the same with all the food in the last month. However hungry men were, after they had been on the peninsula for some time the sight of apricot jam nauseated them, and I believe a large part of the sickness was down to food.

What seems a small detail such as the above, assumes very much larger proportions: the lack of vegetables, the scantiness of bread, the scarcity of water and its quality, all contributed to the ultimate fate of the expeditionary force in the Dardanelles. I cannot help feeling that a little more ingenuity about the food supplied to the troops would have saved us a lot of casualties. Even if redcurrant jam costs more than apricot, the difference in price cannot be a hundredth part of what a large number of casualties cost the nation.

What the Dardanelles expedition has cost us, I tremble to think. I am talking of cash, but what is far more serious is the cost in human life. Did you read Tennant's statement in the House of Commons? From that I calculate that even supposing we say 1,000 of those missing will be found (a very liberal estimate) there were 35,000 deaths on the peninsula and what about the number who died at Lemnos, Alexandria, Malta and at home who died as a consequence of their having been in the Dardanelles?

Suvla
Ours the vain splendour of a high Empire
And the despair of valour vainly spent
Theirs the fulfilment and the long content
Of triumph otherwhere and otherwise
And theirs to see afar with happy eyes
Foam breaking on the verge of Victory
Edward Cadogan

December 1915 – March 1917

Egypt
and North Africa

Editors' notes:

After evacuation from Gallipoli, Cadogan was posted to Egypt. Egypt was the British centre of operations for the campaigns in the East Mediterranean, Africa and the Middle East. The Suez Canal was vital for transport and communication links, and was pivotal to the continued viability of the British Empire. To the north and east of Egypt lay the Ottoman Empire: Palestine at this time was in enemy hands, and just across the Red Sea were the Turkish-held lands that we now know as Yemen and Saudi Arabia.

Save for the odd skirmish, Egypt was the stage for little battle action. Earlier on in the war an enemy force that was sent to attempt the capture or destruction of the Suez Canal had been successfully defeated. However, a repeat attempt remained a possibility. Another perceived threat was posed by certain groups of roaming desert tribes who, it was thought, had been infiltrated by German and Turkish agents sent to stir up dissent and incite revolt against the British.

Apart from the relatively small number of troops engaged in protection and pacification, Egypt's main role was as a staging post for troops and supplies that were to be sent to battle zones nearby.

We left Mudros on about the 19th December, 1915, and we fetched up in the harbour at Alexandria on the morning of the 22nd. They kept us waiting all day long and at about 6 o'clock we disembarked. We had a long march through the town to the train station at Ramleh, which was an awful walk for us and I only just managed to keep going. The train took us about six miles along the coast to a place called Sidi Bishr. Here we had to walk another mile through deep sand to the Yeomanry base camp. It was misery; it felt as if somebody was pushing me back the whole time.

We found tents waiting for us and Herbert Musher in charge. I shared his tent. It came on to blow at night (we were right by the sea) and Herbert M. had to fix the tent, which threatened to collapse. I tried to get up and help but I was so weak I couldn't.

When day broke the next morning we found we were in a most delightful spot with the dark blue sea on one side and the yellow desert, dotted with palm trees on the other. It quite cheered me.

On Christmas day morning we had a Holy Communion service in the mess hut by the sea. Musher took me over to lunch with Lady Howard de Walden at her hospital where I met Lady Elcho, but I was so altered in appearance that she did not recognize me. I was nothing but skin and bone and bright yellow all over and getting worse every day. My thumb and lip began to swell and go black and there were two small pieces of metal in my flesh from the periscope which had been shot whilst I was holding it. Musher arranged with Lady Howard de Walden that I should go in to her officers' hospital.

Taken the day after my return from the Dardanelles. I was so ill (with jaundice!) that I could hardly stand. I was taken to Lady Howard de Walden's hospital, where I spent a week or two in bed. I was then given sick leave and sent up the Nile to recuperate

On the 19th January I was reported fit to leave hospital and was permitted to convalesce in Mervyn Herbert's house in Cairo: number 8 Zamalek, Gezireh. A charming house which he shared with two of his colleagues from the Diplomatic Service (Hugh Thomas and John Cecil) and Lord and Lady Elcho (Letty Manners). She made a delightful hostess. It was a most peaceful and delightful four days that I spent there. On the first day I explored the town and had a look at the glorious view of the desert from the Citadel. That night we left for the High Commissioner's shooting camp, about 40 miles out of Cairo, near Ekiad. Here we found the most luxurious camp and had a splendid duck shoot the following day. We shot 170 duck. It was a most delightful spot among *jheels* on the edge of the desert. We returned to Cairo that afternoon.

Shooting party arriving at Ekiad

Beater amid the jheels

Camp at Ekiad

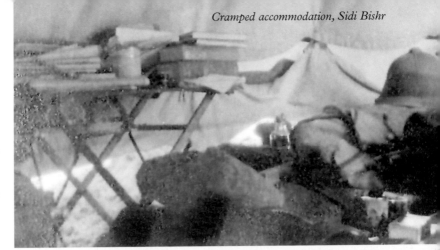
Cramped accommodation, Sidi Bishr

At first I shared a tent with Frank Goldsmith but later on I bought him out, that is to say that together we bought a tent in the town and he inhabited this, leaving me in solitary possession of the other.

My tent, Sidi Bishr

DO NOT EXPOSE TO SUN
OR STOP HEAT LONG ...
CAPT. CADOGAN
SUFFOLK YEOMANRY

Morning drill

I had a thoroughly enjoyable time in camp at Sidi Bishr. Our daily round was very peaceful – about a couple of hours drill in the morning, varied by an occasional route march.

Troops at Sidi Bishr

We sometimes had parades
in the afternoon. If not, I
generally went into Alexandria,
and for the first month nearly
always dined there. It was such
a luxury dining in a hotel
restaurant. We were also
allowed to use the clubs. One
day Frank Goldsmith took me
to see the Jewish Quarter. It
was most interesting as there
were refugees from all parts of
the East – some very venerable-
looking gentlemen from
Bokhara dressed in biblical
garments like Moses and
Aaron.

Camp at Sidi Bishr

Gradually Sidi Bishr became filled with troops. Camps sprang up in every direction and that bit of sea coast between the terminus of the tram station and Aboukir Bay was an extraordinary sight. At one time there must have been between 30,000 and 40,000 troops there.

Sidi Bishr – camps sprung up in every direction

I went to Cairo and spent the night with Mervyn Herbert. The following night I left for Aswan, which I reached on the following evening. In the train I met a man call Sir Hutchinson Poe, who was on the Gordon Relief Expedition and was next to Sir Herbert Stewart when he died. I saw the first mirage I had ever seen from the train window, it was a wonderful counterfeit of a lake. At Aswan I stayed at a small hotel called the St James'. All the big ones were shut. The weather was lovely though very hot. Touring as an officer in such a wonderful country, with no American or any other kind of tourist to mar it, was an ideal way of seeing this part of Egypt.

On the Monday morning I rode five miles across the desert to the reservoir to see Philae. I saw the famous quarries on the way. The Temple of Philae was almost under water. We rowed round it and then proceeded in our boat to see the dam, which is wonderful. I sailed down after lunch (very hot) to Elephantine Island. I then went up to Gordon's Fort to see the sun set, and remained sitting on a high rock above the Nile until it was dark – a delightful evening.

Temple of Philae – submerged by the waters of the Nile after the construction of the Aswan dam

The next day I left for Luxor, which I reached in the late afternoon and I stayed at the Luxor Hotel. The Winter Palace was then a hospital, crammed with soldiers convalescing. I found the Sergeant of my old Bury troops there. Chops Ramsden and Redmond Buxton were at Luxor and I went with them at night to see the Temple of Karnak by the light of the moon. Except the Taj Mahal under similar circumstances, I don't think I have ever seen anything more impressive. The next day I had a hard day's sightseeing at the Tomb of the Kings and the Plain of Thebes. That night I went to see the Temple of Luxor by moonlight. Chops Ramsden had an awful fall – he stepped on thin air thinking it was *terra firma* and fell down about six foot. Luckily no bones broken. The next day I renewed my acquaintance with Karnak and that evening left for Cairo. When I woke in the train the next morning I had a wonderful view of the pyramids, only their tops were showing out of a white, morning mist and they were coral in colour.

Karnak Temple, Luxor

Winter Palace Hotel, Luxor, 1916 used as a hospital

Camp at El Kubri

On the 25th February I rejoined my regiment at Sidi Bishr. On the 16th March we received orders to pack up and proceed to a place called El Kubri – a camp in the desert, east of the canal and just north of Suez.

I had a return of jaundice and consequently had a very bad time on the journey. However, I soon got fit again and enjoyed my time. It was real, yellow desert. Our camp was very well-pitched with plenty of tents and elbow space. It was close to the canal. We did a lot of riding in the desert. I had an awfully nice little mare, which went like the wind.

The evenings were perfectly glorious. Our energies at this time were employed in putting the canal in a state of defence, making wire entanglements etc.

Suffolk Yeomen riding out from El Kubri, 1916

Along with desert-riding, we organised other sports in our spare time such as high-jump competitions and running races

Below: Being only 160 strong, when we landed in Egypt and having to wait a long while for reinforcements, we were turned on to light jobs such as wiring the Suez Canal

Frank Goldsmith, El Kubri

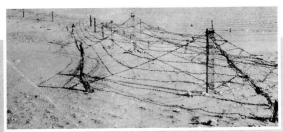

Suffolk Yeomanry, Port Tewfik

On exercise

*Trains of
mules kicked
up dust*

Desert training

The weather was now getting tremendously hot, but I did not mind it as the heat was dry. Sand-storms are the trouble in camp. In May, the whole of the 42nd Division received orders to concentrate at Port Tewfik. This was a much more trying camp than El Kubri. It was terribly crowded, a very dirty bit of desert, next to the Sweetwater Canal, which had been frequently used for camps before. The dust is awful. Not the clean dust of the desert, but dirty, incinerator dust. At intervals during the day the train of mules passed our tents to water and each time we were treated to a dense mist of dust which stank. It was a horrible spot. We did a certain amount of training while there. What the reason of our being there was I never quite discerned, but Charlie Harding told me he thought that trouble was anticipated in India and that we were to go off there if required. We were under the command of a man called Douglas. The soldiers had another name for him. How that man could ever have reached the rank of divisional general I could not conceive. He was a dud. Even the military authorities found it out and bowlered him eventually. He insisted on holding an enormous review in the hot plain-mouth of Suez. I never saw such a show. He tried to make the dismounted Yeomanry come past the saluting point last. Our Brigadier went to him and told him that if the cavalry did not go past in their proper place they would not march past him at all. This announcement brought him to his so-called senses. On one occasion he delivered a lecture to the Yeomanry officers – the subject being 'How to be an officer and a gentleman at the same time.' Two subjects on which I should think he himself must have been completely ignorant.

Marching in formation

Clutterbuck

Walter Guinness was back as second-in-command and young Clutterbuck became the Adjutant. I was more than ever confirmed in my opinion as to what a good fellow the latter was.

Herbert Musher – who was also going on leave – and I, went into Port Tewfik and slept the night there on the 17th May. The next morning we boarded the P&O and we proceeded up the Suez Canal. The banks of the canal were one mass of encampments, mainly Australian, and the whole canal was full of naked men bathing. At Port Said the following passengers came on board: Lady Elcho, whose husband had just been killed at Katia, although she was ignorant of this at the time, Mrs Charlie Coventry, whose husband had been taken prisoner there, Lady May Strickland and Edward Homer, who was killed later in France, and Willie Percy. We formed a cheerful party for the journey.

West Kent Yeomanry, Suez Canal

Self going to Port Tewfik to embark for home leave, summer 1916

The canal at El Firdan

I stayed the night at the San Stephano Hotel where I met Guy Wilson. On the next day I sought out my regiment, which I found encamped on the banks of the canal at El Firdan, not far south of Kantara. We were supposed to be returning to Sidi Bishr, but owing to the Turkish attack at Katia we were told to wait. One morning we were told to parade in full marching order and to be prepared to move at a moment's notice. This looked like real business. But the order was cancelled when we had got ourselves ready! The weather was very hot and our chief amusement was bathing in the canal. Not long after my return I had a bad go of fever. I sent for our doctor Taylor, a good man, but not a very good physician. I felt on fire, but for some reason he did not take my temperature. That night I had such a raging fit of delirium that some of my brother officers, who were playing bridge just outside my tent, had to move away! I never felt so queer in my life. I remember watching the huge liners coming within a few yards of my tent, which was pitched absolutely on the bank of the canal. That, when you are not *compos* is a terrifying apparition. The next morning my Colonel came in to see me and took my temperature – it was 104°, so what it must have been the night before I tremble to think. As soon as I was well enough to travel I was sent off to Alexandria, where I stayed in the delightful San Stephano Hotel by the sea until I was well. In the meantime the regiment had been sent off to the Western Desert of Egypt to keep the Senussi quiet.

I watched the huge liners coming within a few yards of my tent

Our chief amusement was bathing in the canal – Woods and Limmington playing at boats

Form 1 — Transport de Troupes

MARSEILLE-JOLIETTE

Gare expé ditrice — *Boulogne Nord*
Gare destinataire
Compagnie destinataire

P.L.M. — Grande Vitesse

Direct — 17/2 — 220913

TRANSPORT DE TROUPES

effectué ... chemin de fer N° 15-16

délivré ...

BILLET COLLECTIF N°

Pour le transport d'un détachement *d'un officier anglais*

commandé par

	OFFICIERS	OFFICIERS	HOMMES de troupe		PLACES				TOTAL
HOMMES		1							
1re classe									
2e classe									
3e classe									

CHEVAUX — CHEVAUX D'OFFICIERS / CHEVAUX et MULETS de troupe / CHEVAUX et MULETS de trait pour voitures / ANIMAUX

BAGAGES — Poids total: 62 Kil. — 2 colis

MATÉRIEL

OFFICIERS

Hommes ayant droit à un cheval
Conducteurs

MOVEMENT ORDER — Army Form W. 3039.

Form 2 — Messages and Signals

"A" Form — **MESSAGES AND SIGNALS.** — Army Form C. 2121.

No. of Message

Office of Origin and Service Instructions — Prefix — Code — Words — Charge

This message is on a/c of:
Sent — At ... m. — To ... By ... (Signature of "Franking Officer.")
Recd. at ... m. — Date — From — By

TO **3rd Dismounted Brigade**

Sender's Number **A222/104** — Day of Month — In reply to Number — AAA

G.H.Q. wires one months leave
from date of Embarkation approved
Capt Hon Edward J Cadogan and
Lieut H Meysey 4/1 Suffolk
Yeomanry

Certified that P&O s/s "MOOLTAN"
left Port Said on 20th May 1916.
... Nurses.

Certified true copy
... Kavanagh Capt
Bde Major
3rd Dismounted Bde

Form 3 — Movement Order

MOVEMENT ORDER — Army Form W. 3039.

A222/104 — 11-5-16 — Date 25/5/16

Train No. ...

| Designation of Despatching Unit or Service | Officers | Other Ranks | Sick and wounded men | Prisoners of war | Horses | | Vehicles | | | | Miscellaneous No. of packages | Track loads | Track Numbers | From | To |
| 1 | 2 | 3 | 4 | 5 | 6 Riding | 7 Draught | 8 | 9 | 10 | 11 | 12 | | 13 | 14 | 15 |

Capt Hon Cadogan
4/1 Suffolk Yeo
on leave
travelling free

Approved by BdC

Marseilles — United Kingdom via Boulogne

Signed — Officer Authorising Move.
Signed — Officer in Charge of Train.
Signed — R.T.O. Despatching Station.

RECONSIGNED.

| From | To | Signature of R.T.O. |

(1174.) Wt. 3645-1497. 10,000 10/15. H.C.& L. Ltd.

Movement order form used on 25th May, 1916 for home leave

I rejoined the regiment at a place called Dabaa, some 150 miles west of Alexandria. It was a very delightful spot, for those who do not object to being in the wilderness.

Pemberton bathing

Its chief redeeming feature was that it was near the sea – and a wonderful sea coast it is there. Snow-white sand and sapphire sea – perfect for bathing.

My regiment was in this camp for over six months and I am not sure, looking back upon it, that they were not the pleasantest months of the war. It was a roughish life but it had its advantages. We were very rarely badgered by generals or inspecting officers and although we were in enemy country our life was peaceful. It was extraordinarily healthy: we rode most of the day and bathed. We had a much larger measure of freedom in every way than we had enjoyed since the war began and the climate was perfect. The disadvantages were that we were so out of the way, we had but little leave and besides ourselves there was only a squadron of Hertfordshire Yeomanry.

Everyday life at Dabaa – drawing water

Petulant camel

The Senussi were quite friendly

Time passed pleasantly enough at Dabaa. At first we were told that no officer must ever ride out into the desert by himself and he must always be armed to the teeth. But I soon found that the Senussi were quite friendly – they were too starved to be anything else, and I used to ride all over the place by myself. Whenever I met any of them I used to ride up to them and give them cigarettes. Knowing no Arabic it was the only way I had of showing them I was not an oppressor!

Self and Clutterbuck on one of our many rides

The memory which clings to me most of these pleasant days at Dabaa is that of our rides after foxes up on the hilly ground. The going was perfect. It is not like the yellow, sandy desert of the Sahara, but the browner earth more like English dust. In the summer it is arid, but in the spring it is a mass of flowers. Clutterbuck was my companion on most of these rides and we became the very best of friends. I had a wonderful mare, very fast, but unfortunately none too sound, and the gallops over the desert were sometimes a little too much for her. It was glorious riding back to camp in the cool of the evening with the sun setting into the sea, as only it knows how in Egypt.

Pet dog, tent and hut in background, Dabaa 1916

I had never been much of a swimmer before this experience, but I became quite proficient owing to so much of our spare time at Dabaa being spent in the water. Our camp consisted of tents and a hut or two. The perimeter was surrounded by terrific barbed wire entanglements and there were two strong posts which were really forts cut in the rock, which we used to man every night.

At the railhead

The place was at the rail head and there was an Egyptian police barracks close-by. On the other side of the railway was a huge barbed wire enclosure where the Senussi, who had become friendly, could pitch their tents and buy food from us.

Hunting wild dogs

We suffered terribly from wild dogs at Dabaa. They are night animals and the howling and yelling that went on after dark in and around our camp was awful. I used to have shots at them with a scatter gun. The men used to set traps for them and then bayonet them, giving as an excuse for this cruelty that it was good bayonet practice. We have got some dogs from Alexandria and we used to hunt the wild dogs in the daytime on our horses. They sometimes gave us great sport.

To amuse ourselves we staged shows

Stage erected for event, Dabaa, August and September, 1916

We kept ourselves amused...

Golf

Tennis

Tug-o'-war

The station master's house

Trench on Tomb Hill

Self (left) and Pemberton riding camels

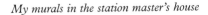

My murals in the station master's house

In November I was sent with my squadron (I was still in command of A Squadron) to garrison two places, called respectively: Hamman and Amrieh. I had my headquarters at Hamman in the station master's bothy. It was a desolate spot and I was frightfully bored there. I had only one other officer with me and an RAMC doctor. There was a system of trenches dug round the place. When they were dug some very interesting Roman remains were come upon - a series of arches which looked like catacombs. The whole of this country is a mass of Roman remains. It was here that Anthony and Cleopatra lived – somewhere on this coast. But the interest of the Roman remains was not enough to alleviate the boredom of that place. Luckily Egyptian police from the barracks on the other side of the line used to lend me their little, white Sudanese camels, which are very comfortable to ride. In my spare time I painted some murals in the station master's house in the style of the tombs of the Kings at Luxor – so hard put to it I was for a job! It was while I was at Hamman that news came of Germany's first overtures of peace – November 1916. It filled me with hope, but not for very long when I realized what their terms were.

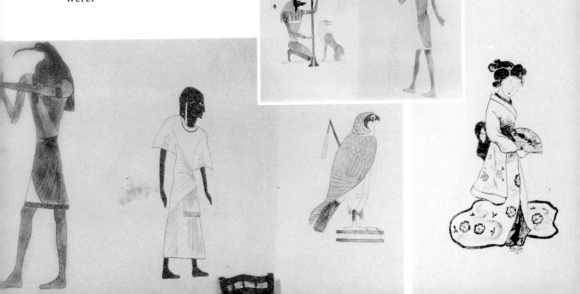

Our flooded camp, Christmas 1916

I went back with my squadron to Dabaa just before Christmas and soon after my return there the rains began and absolutely turned our camp into a lake. We had ordered a mass of turkeys for the men's dinner. They came up by train from Alexandria and expired of some foul disease as soon as they arrived at Dabaa. This was a terrible blow to us all!

Clutterbuck with another member of the Suffolk
Yeomany and a dead turkey

Pass to Alexandria

In January, 1917, the weather cleared and then the country took on the most gorgeous aspect. I could not have believed that so arid a desert could be so quickly transformed into an absolute garden. The wild flowers in that part of the world at that season are beyond all belief.

In February, I went for two or three days leave and spent them with an old Balliol friend, Mahmoud (then *Mudir* of Damanhur). He had a very nice residence in Damanhur and he sent me and Geoffrey Barker, who had accompanied me, out duck shooting. We had tea with an *omda* of a native village which was an amusing experience. Only one member of the family, the nephew of the *omda*, could talk broken-English. I remember when we tried to tip the beaters, he protested in the following terms: 'If you do *dat*, my uncle he become very sorry.'

With the arrival of spring at Dabaa came a warning that we should shortly be wanted on much more active service than we had recently had to endure. There were several indications that something was going to happen. Instructors in infantry drill were sent to us and 12 new officers arrived without warning.

Then came our definite marching orders – we were to proceed to Alexandria once more, there to refit as an infantry regiment. Farewell then to all our fond hopes of being turned back into cavalry again.

When we arrived at Alexandria we were told to proceed to Sidi Bishr where they put us in camp not far from our old quarters. We received an enormous draft to bring us up to infantry strength – mostly veterans from France, excellent men. Under the re-organisation I was selected as Company Commander and placed in command of A Company.

April 1917 – November 1918

Palestine

Editors' notes:

After a few weeks in Alexandria, Cadogan and his men received orders for the front. They were to form part of the force attempting to take Palestine and Jerusalem from the Turks.

The British Campaign in Palestine had a three-pronged approach. Firstly, by advancing the front line further from Egypt it decreased the threat to the Suez Canal from an attack across the Sinai. Secondly, it was thought that the presence of even a small British force could encourage and support the dissatisfied native Arab population to insurrection against the occupying Turks. This would then tie up a disproportionate amount of Turkish troops, further weakening the combative strength of one of the Axis powers. Thirdly, and most importantly, was the ideological significance of capturing the prize of Jerusalem. Wresting control of the Holy City away from 'the infidels' would be a massive moral boost to allied troops and correspondingly be detrimental to the moral of the enemy.

The railway alongside the Suez canal

On Sunday 7th April – Easter Day – we set off at 3am in the morning for Palestine. We reached Kantara on the Suez Canal in the afternoon.

After a time we were ordered out of the train and marched across the Suez Canal up into Kantara, which had been converted into a vast camp for the invading army. After we had given our men food at a canteen we marched up to the station where we waited for hours. We were told that the officers would have a sleeping car. Visions of the Great Northern Scottish Express flitted across my brain, which were rudely dispelled by the reality, which turned out to be a long wagon with trays at the side; fearfully drafty and dirty. Into this we packed, and after dark the train started off north.

Desert kit inspection

When we were about at El Arish, and had dozed off into our first sweet sleep, someone opened the door of our carriage and said: 'There's a hotbox on one of the wagons behind, they are unhooking it and if you are not careful the wagon with all your kits in it will be left behind in a siding.' I kicked up Limmington (one of my subalterns) out of a heavy sleep and with him we roused as many NCOs and men as possible, to come and manhandle all the kits out of the rear wagons, which had been unhooked and put into a siding. When day broke we were well into Palestine.

The whole division was bivouacking in a dense mass and German planes were hovering over us. The country all round was rather attractive at that time of the year. It had not yet been devastated by the tramp of advancing armies, and on the undulating hills the crops made it look not unlike Berkshire or Sussex. We did not put up any tents, the weather was so perfect it would have been a waste of time and trouble, but I did rig up my camp bed.

On Thursday 12th April I received orders to proceed to the Wadi Guzzi with a number of men and supervise making a water dump. Although the *wadi* was dry there was a spring at this point and we had to build horse troughs etc.

While my men were at work in the *wadi* I clambered up the far side on to the bank, which was really no man's land at the time, and had a look at the country we were about to attack. It consisted of a long, low range of hills which protected the line Gaza – Beersheba.

Camel Corps on the move (trench in foreground)

Saturday, 14th April

After we had had breakfast in our camp at Belah, the enemy suddenly started shelling. They began by shelling the hospital tents with large, high explosives. One of my brother officers, Leslie, had ridden over there to get some dressings, and was standing by the side of his horse waiting for them when one of these shells landed almost onto his horse, smashed it to bits and wounded Leslie in seven places! Then they started shelling the ground in front of our camp – a large number of the Egyptian labour corps with their camels happened to be crossing this bit of ground at the time and it was amusing to watch them scatter. We all hastily dug holes in the ground. Mercifully no shells pitched among us as we were so densely packed they would have done us infinite damage.

In the evening I had orders to spend the night on outpost duty. In other words, take my squadron out into no man's land and dig some extemporary trenches, the idea being to prevent enemy parties coming through our lines. Brigadier McNill came out with us. We had to march through a sort of defile, which the Tommies call Piccadilly Circus, and down to the Wadi Guzzi. I had to gallop on ahead with the Colonel so as to get to the position before the sun had set entirely so we could examine the nature of the ground. My position was just across the *wadi* – but I had not much time to learn

Camel Corps resting

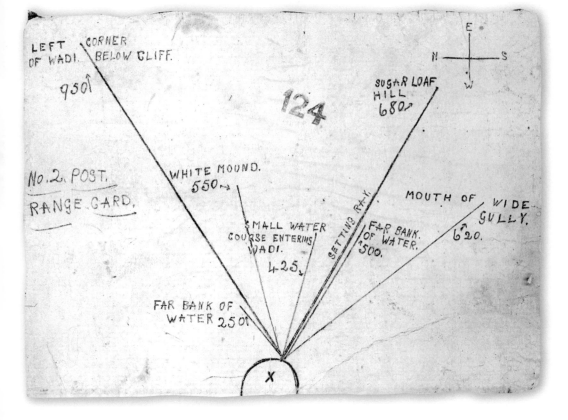

Trench charts

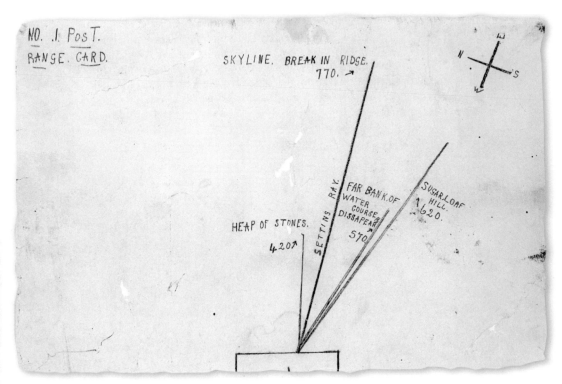

the geography. While I was doing so, I looked back and saw my men coming over the hill. The sun was setting behind them and making their dust, which is awful in this part of the world, very distinct, and I can't understand why the Turk did not shell them as they must have been in full view of the sentries' posts. However, darkness closed in upon us and we set to work on our trenches. No incident – and we returned to camp at daybreak.

Monday, 16th April

In the afternoon I had orders to take up an outpost line again. The second attempt on Gaza was about to begin and tonight the Army were to move out into position through our line of outposts.

An orderly came up to me somewhere out of the darkness with a message to say that all the officers senior to me had been sent off on various jobs and that I was to go back to Regimental Headquarters and to take command of the regiment in the meantime.

I groped my way back to the Wadi Guzzi where I had left my batman and horse. Having found him I mounted and proceeded along the dried up river-bed to the point where I had been told Regimental Headquarters was situated. I had not been floundering along for many yards when I discovered the army was moving stealthily along the *wadi* too – with camels and everything else, a

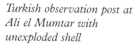

Turkish observation post at Ali el Mumtar with unexploded shell

most impressive sight. I travelled along for some distance thinking I must have lost the way when suddenly I stumbled upon a lot of men sleeping in the bank.

'Who goes there?' Called an angry voice from the ground.

'OC Suffolk Yeomanry.' I replied.

'Are you?' Was the rejoinder, 'I thought I was!'

By a strange coincidence it was Tommy Grissel whom I had stumbled upon. I got off my horse and he explained to me that he had been sent off for another job but that he had been suddenly sent back to take command of the regiment. I told him that he must let me command it until I had something to eat as I was famished! He produced some sardines and having satisfied my hunger I returned back to my outpost line.

Tuesday, 17th April

This was the first day of the second battle of Gaza. All morning we were busy with preparations. I have never seen anything like the amount of things they expect a soldier to carry into battle! Our orders were in a most awful state of confusion thanks to the Adjutant having held them up and then passing them to us *en masse*. It was impossible to grasp their contents in the short time available to us. I am amazed how some sort of order evolved out of the chaos. In just a few hours we were ready. We then marched out over the rolling plains towards the Wadi Guzzi.

Our destination this day was a ridge beyond Piccadilly Circus where the regiment bivouacked for the day in battle reserve. This ridge commanded a magnificent view from the sea round to Gaza and the large amphitheatre of hills which stretched from Gaza to Tel el Yemmi (a high feature in the landscape). These hills were the objective of the day's fighting.

In the evening my regiment orders were to advance so, just as the sun set, we started off and marched in the direction of the Sheikh el Abbas ridge. The REs had prepared the country for us – there were innumerable signposts telling us where there was water, where the crossings over the *wadi* were to be found, which were the crossings for artillery and which were for cavalry. There were bridges everywhere and a very good effort had been made at re-paving, or rather making roads, which are practically non-existent in the Turkish Empire. There were boards with large numbers on them dotted about, which corresponded with numbers on our maps which, by the way, were very deficient. The march was slow – the track being bad – and we were constantly passing other troops. The dust was awful: we marched in a fog of it. We wore drill with shorts, a kit which gets clammy in the daytime heat and freezing at night. It was an awful march. On Wednesday 18th April at 1am or 2am we came to a halt and I could see shrapnel bursting in the air ahead of us. There is nothing so weird as shrapnel, or other shells, bursting at night. As day broke we found ourselves in open fields, a high sort of platform surrounded by hilly country. We were formed up into review order and told to lie down and get what rest we could.

Thursday, 19th April

We had little or no sleep, and got the regiment on the march in the dark, early hours, and then started off. The Colonel thought he knew the way. We had been going for some time when we discovered we were marching round and round in a circle. We began to laugh and the Colonel began to swear – but it was no laughing matter as the day was coming up and we might easily have been caught on the track leading up to the ridge if a tank had espied us. Luckily this did not happen and just as the sun came up over the hills I arrived with my company on the top of Sheikh el Abbas ridge, a portion of which had been wrested from the enemy the day before. Here I found the Brigadier who told me to tuck my company well into the leeward side of the ridge as the enemy would probably start shelling us. The Brigadier was a model of calmness. Shortly after I had obeyed this order the Colonel came fuming up the hill shouting at me 'Captain Cadogan! Why the devil have you put your company in here?' My reason was such an excellent one and so conclusive that he had to retire muttering in a state of baffled discontent. Having ensconced my company I went up with the Adjutant to the ridge, which had a good view of the advancing troops and a nice little bank to duck down under whenever the enemy shelled us with shrapnel – which they did at intervals throughout the day. One of the first shells that burst over us wounded Sergeant Smith of my company. The battle began soon after sunrise.

The ridge

The Brigadier Major was constantly receiving messages. One was to the effect that the enemy was showing signs of liveliness on our right flank, so I had to detach a post from my company to watch it. From what we could make out, the cavalry were not making good on the flank – so our situation was becoming serious. General Murray sent orders that the 74th Division was to attack and take Ali el Mumtar – the big feature close to Gaza – at dawn the next day. But three of the Divisional Commanders, hearing how hopelessly the attack on Gaza had already failed, and at what an appalling loss of troops, absolutely declined. Had they carried out Murray's orders, I can only imagine that the rest of his army would have been cut to pieces. We would have had no reserves and one of the most disastrous defeats would have ensued. Early the following morning the Brigadier got a telegram from GHQ saying 'Cancel orders', or words to that effect.

On the retreat after 2nd Battle of Gaza

We were weary and sick at heart when we commenced our march retrogressively. An army in retreat is not a cheerful affair. We came into a shelter of a very narrow *wadi* where the sun's rays beat down on us mercilessly. We had not been moving long when a German tank appeared and hovered over us. I noticed that it turned round twice. A minute afterwards we had some enemy shells over us, but the target was a narrow one and no-one was injured. The tank shot at us with a machine gun but with no effect. At last we emerged into the open. We had been going uphill for some distance and found ourselves on a kind of plateau. I afterwards discovered we had come round in a circle and a march which had taken us all the morning ought only to have taken us about an hour. So much for our young guide's perspicacity and genius for map reading!

I thought our march was never going to end. We stumbled on until we came under cover of a convenient ridge which was cut up into numerous valleys and corries. We were told to dig ourselves some sort of protection and to have a much needed rest. We decided that as we had no blankets the best plan was to dig a large square hole and lie in a heap together to obtain some reciprocal warmth, for the cold at night was so intense. Then word reached us that the Turk was going to follow up his advantage and attack. We were given orders about a counter-attack. Night came on without any further instructions reaching us, but one did not feel particularly at ease when our main body had been defeated. Nevertheless, sleep was absolutely essential. The cold was perishing. There was a heavy dew which made matters worse. We had some waterproof sheets but used as quilts they are worse than nothing at all. It is wonderful how little sleep one can do if put to it. Over the last five days campaigning we have only had a few hours.

Gaza town can just be made out on the horizon

After the battle there ensued a period of about 90 days, during which neither side seemed to display any desire to take the initiative. It was not exactly guerrilla warfare, it was more like a game of hide and seek. Until General Sir Archibald Murray – who I never saw once during the whole time I was on the Palestine front – was suspended by Lord Allenby, there appeared to be no plan of campaign whatever. We were a forgotten army. Both sides settled down to inactivity – their relations almost friendly. I remember there was a gentlemen's agreement not to shoot each other while we were sea-bathing. The men were in far better spirits than they were at Gallipoli. There was far more elbow room and variety of occupation. Also, we were not continually under fire, although there was intermittent shelling, sufficient to remind us that we were on the front line. The opposing forces were rarely very far apart. By the 25th April we had dug to such effect that we had prepared a regular trench system, which could be of some use in the event of an attack.

One night I was roused in the small hours by a loud rumbling noise on the opposite side of the *wadi*. This was followed by shouting and much running to and fro. It was pitch-dark when I emerged from my dug-out to see what was the matter. An accident had just taken place. The cliff-like side of the *wadi* had collapsed and buried three of our men under the debris. I ran to fetch the doctor while my men dug like fury. It was a grim scene when I came back with him. By the light of one or two flickering candles the men of my company were working for all they were worth to save their comrades. Every now and then there was a shout of 'Here's an arm' or 'Here's a leg'. Then the digging would be renewed with re-doubled fury. We found two of them alive, although badly bruised and suffering from shock. The other was dead and he showed no sign of reaction to the doctor's persistence in working his arms and chest. It was a tragic moment when he gave it up as a bad job. The victim came from Ipswich. His name was Scrivener curiously enough, as I was told he could neither read nor write. The next day Frank Goldsmith and I took the body of the poor man in a cart and buried him in a sort of garden surrounded by cactus and overlooking a magnificent view of the countryside.

Cactus surrounding the garden where Scrivener is buried

I rode about the country on my horse whenever I had spare time

Canteen wagon

Our brigade now received orders to move a good long way forth down the line in a south easterly direction. We were bound for the Shellal lines, which had previously been occupied by the Turk. As usual, the enemy showed no signs of attempting to dislodge us once we were dug in. We stayed there for some days. It was here that I had my first experience of enemy bombing – a very poor effort as it proved to be. When the plane was directly over us it dropped a bomb. It seemed to take a very long time falling and it fell quite some 40 yards away with a good deal of noise. There followed some days of routine work. I rode about the country on my horse whenever I had any spare time. We were fairly comfortable as far as food was concerned as the railway had already advanced almost up to our trench line. Where there were railheads there were always canteen tents where such luxuries as tinned fruits could be procured to relieve the monotony of bully beef and biscuits.

H. Wood, Barker and self at Tel el Fara

On the 12th May I received orders to take my company out to hold the advanced line at a place called Tel el Fara which featured an interesting hill rising abruptly out of the plain. It had evidently been used as a burial ground by some prehistoric race. We came upon human skulls when we were digging, also stone coffins and cinerary urns. Our line of trenches and dumps (formerly Turkish) lay on the nearside of a *wadi*. On the first night just as I turned in to my dug-out a signaller dashed up with an urgent message to the effect that the Turks were expected to attack in small parties and endeavour a crossing of the *wadi*. I was rather out in the air with my company and I had no definite orders at all as to what I was expected to do in the event of these contingencies materialising. My only orders were to get onto the Brigadier Major by means of the field telephone. After two hours of anxiously trying to contact the

Brigadier Major I eventually got on to him. All he said was to make my men stand to for a while. For some hours I walked up and down the line. After a few hours and nothing much doing I took one or two extra precautions and ordered my men to lie down.

In the afternoon of the following day a signaller came up to me with a message from my Colonel that the Turks had crossed the *wadi*. In accordance with my instructions, I rang up the Brigadier Major for orders. I then discovered that the Colonel had been practising with his signallers and that this was a dummy message. He had forgotten to record this rather important fact on the telegraph form. The Colonel was furious and described my action in ringing up the Brigadier Major as unnecessary fuss. Apart from the fact that I was obeying orders I should have thought it was unnecessary carelessness on the Colonel's part not writing 'dummy' on the erring form!

We had orders to re-occupy the Sheikh el Abbas ridge and we arrived at our destination soon after midnight after a desperate march. It was a weird looking place; rather like a corrie in a Scotch deer forest, except for the fact that the whole place was riddled with dug-outs, saps and dumps. When I arrived with my company I sought out the Company Commander of our predecessors and found him, and one or two others, in their dug-outs. They were in a nervous condition as they had a terrible shelling the night before – some thousand shells had fallen in the area. While I was talking with them two bullets whizzed through the air. The officers almost fell on their faces. On the following morning I had time to look about me. It certainly was not a pleasant pitch. My company was accommodated in the dry river-bed, which served us for the purpose of both protection and a sap up to our trenches, which were situated on the stay line. It was a stiff climb. From our trenches we had a magnificent view of the surrounding country, but if the Turk had only had his wits about him he could have made our position untenable. We could be shelled from our front.

There was no water where we were encamped. It had to be brought up by camels at night. A string of these animals used to come stealthily passed my dug-out in the dark – the fantasises making a soft bell-like sound as they flapped against the camels' sides.

One of the most gruelling features of the place was that our guns were mounted not far behind us. To me they sounded as if they were only a few yards away. At intervals all through the night they let off salvos, which seemed powerful enough to blow me out of my dug-out.

I was sent off to conduct a signalling class on a great plain between the enemy lines and our own. A telephone cable connected us with the Colonel's headquarters. One morning we were subjected to a couple of shrapnel shells. I got my men into a fold in the ground, the only shelter available, and telephoned to the Colonel our predicament. He replied in terms that suggested it was only my imagination. I could not make out what he meant. Anyone who has ever been subjected to a shower of shrapnel is not likely to mistake it for anything else. But he told me to bring my men in and once again hinted that I was allowing my imagination to run loose. The words were hardly out of his mouth when the enemy sent over another dose of shrapnel almost onto the Colonel's dug-out. I must say he saw the joke and apologised to me.

Kit inspections, drill in a very cramped area, bomb throwing practices, and the inspection of trenches formed the average occupation in the daytime. Every afternoon

Lieutenant Hankey (Cheshire Regiment) standing in shell hole

Signalling in the desert

From our trenches we had a magnificent view of the surrounding country

about four o'clock our aeroplanes crossed the enemy line and the enemy aeroplanes cross ours, to the accompaniment of terrific shelling from both sides. Often enough there were air-battles over our heads. Why some of us were not killed by the falling metal from anti-aircraft shells I cannot understand. It used to come down in showers. We had no headcover as timber was unprocurable. We counted 200 shells fired at one aeroplane alone. Overall, our sojourn in the pitch lasted about five weeks.

On the 4th June we mustered all the old Etonians we could find in the brigade. We contrived a quite luxurious supper on a kind of plateau behind the trenches, which was, in fact, well under fire. Machine guns could easily reach it and certainly shells. But our devotion to the old school outstripped our discretion. It was a romantic setting for the celebration of the great Eton anniversary. The food was a triumph considering our circumstances. I remember particularly a lobster salad, which was indeed a luxury in those days. We decided to send a telegram to the Headmaster which somebody translated into Latin. I can recollect only three words of it 'Apud portas Gazae'! [1]

Article from Chin Wag – Eton *school paper*

The Palestine News, *Thursday, 13 June 1918*

1 It did in fact translate as: '28 Etonians from the Gates of Gaza send greetings'

An inter-regimental football match

On the last day of June we were holding a line of trenches, at the back of which was a large open space which resembled a football ground. It resembled one so much that our fellows on the other regiments in these trenches decided to convert it to this use and to play some matches. On this particular day an inter-regimental match was in progress, watched by a large crowd, including myself. Just as the match was concluding, the enemy discovered what was happening and opened with shrapnel. Luckily the crowd of onlookers was by this time dispersed, but as there was no head cover anywhere except blankets, the fragments of shell firmly poured down upon us. I don't think anyone was hit – it was lucky the crowd had scattered as the majority of the shells burst with force and precision on the improvised football ground.

The crowd of spectators

On the Saturday, 18th August I was sent off to do a gas course at Tel el Kebir. This was a name which conjured up the days of my childhood. It was given to the battle in which Lord Wellesley made his name and fame in 1882. A number of those who fought it were friends of my parents and I looked upon them with great awe and reverence. It was rather a pleasant change from my dreary life in the wilderness. The gas school consisted of a few huts located close to the old British trenches, which were still intact after an interval of over 30 years. The soil here consists of pebbles and not of sand and as there is hardly any rainfall the battlefield has remained as it was.

Trenches of Tel el Kebir preserved for over 30 years

I was mounted at the head of my company and a real bad mount I had during this campaign. I had to leave behind the mare I liked so much in the Western Desert as I did not think she was sound enough for this sort of job. I had now a brute of the hackney type. She was always getting her feet caught in telephone wires which were laid all over the country, and I should think probably cut all sorts of communications.

We got orders for Belah. This was a long march and when, though only three or four miles from the town, endurance had reached its limit we all lay down by the roadside for a bit of sleep. I was the first to wake. At dawn I roused my men to the

accompaniment of some fairly lurid speech – the language of soldiers on the march is pretty useful. We set off again on our weary tramp. At Belah I received orders to take the men up to the railway station. Drawn up alongside one of the platforms was a train consisting of luggage vans. We were ordered to strip naked and place all our kit in these receptacles that they were disinfecting with a smoke apparatus. It was an intriguing sight: a company of Suffolk Yeoman standing about on the platform – nude, apart from boots and helmets. It was most unpleasant as we had to wait for about two hours in this predicament while a terrible duststorm arose. A dismal dump in a duststorm has to be seen to be believed. It is composed, not of the clean dust of the desert, but of the filth of incinerators and horse lines. We got into a disgusting condition. However, when our clothing was

Normal washing facilities were inadequate to keep clean

restored to us I marched our company down to the sea and enjoyed the most delicious bathe I ever remember.

The beach at Belah was interesting as it was here they were landing all our stores. It somewhat resembled the beach at Anzac. After bathing we repaired to our regimental dump, which was situated on the plain where the 74th Division had originally concentrated before the battle of Gaza. We had a delightful night's sleep under the stars and the next day we returned to Shellah to be greeted by another appalling duststorm, product of the *khamseen* wind. On one occasion I had just turned in, or rather thrown myself on the ground, when it commenced with red fury. I covered

my body with a piece of mosquito net but it soon became intolerable. Goods and chattels were caught up in the wind and whirled away into space; a pith helmet hurtled past me through the air. It was devastating. I could not remain still. It was like a dense fog with driving wind. Frank Goldsmith came and sat with me, both of us looking the picture of misery. We compared notes and it was obvious the limit of endurance of this kind of life had been reached.

The regiment now had orders to proceed to the coast. It was the month of December. I must admit that this billet was a very pleasing one. It was situated on the coast, just south of Gaza. My dug-out was by the sea. It was a wonderful sight at night watching the waves lit up by the flashes of the shells. It was not altogether comfortable as there was a great deal of firing from both sides after dark. As usual we had to dig trenches quite close to enemy lines. I had to march my company up to Samson's Ridge at night. It was a most uncanny job, with only the moon to guide us. It was a great difficulty to induce the men to work quietly at their job. They slapped the sand with their spades and made an awful noise. Why the Turks did not rake us with machine guns I cannot conceive.

There came a day when I was to say farewell to my regiment and it was with a heavy heart that I set off one evening to Belah and on to Cairo. I was feeling completely exhausted.

My dug-out

I reported myself to General Clayton on my arrival. He explained to me my job in the Intelligence Corps. For the present I was to work in the Arab Bureau and then to go up country into Palestine. I did not go up into Palestine until the 27th November – which was after Jerusalem had fallen. I then set off with General Clayton for a camp near Gaza.

The town was now in ruins and the whole country around it was the abomination of desolation. I visited our former trench line at Sheikh el Abbas and walked across the plain where I had watched the failure of our army in the previous spring and I thought of the fate of poor Eustace Cubritt with whom I had struck up a friendship which I had hoped would endure.

Devastion of Gaza

General Clayton was joined by Monsieur Picot, head of the French political mission, who for his country's prestige wanted to be in at the death. I subsequently had a great deal of association with him. He was a tiresome individual who, as so many others of his race, was very anxious that the French should have as much kudos, and incidentally as much territory in the Middle East, as he could claim. It was in this camp that I made the acquaintance of the famous Lawrence of Arabia. He was somewhat disappointing in appearance. He was very short – made all the shorter by the voluminous Arab robes which he habitually affected. I found him rather a *poseur*, but in many ways he was impressive enough. I got on very well with him. It was here too that we were joined by General Wyndham Deedes, with whom I made great friends. He was then a very attractive personality.

Monsieur Picot (French Political Officer)

In December I went to Jaffa and then on to Jerusalem. I was far too depressed to react as I should have done to my first view of the Holy City, but of course, I could not fail to be glad I was at last within its precincts. The view of the walled town from the Mount of Olives was very lovely and there was much in the course of my sightseeing there to fill one with awe and reverence. On Christmas Eve I motored off with George Lloyd (afterwards Governor of Bombay and High Commissioner of Egypt) to Bethlehem to hear mass in the Church of the Nativity. It was the first occasion that the sacred birthplace had ever been in British hands. The church was filled with our soldiers in khaki – a moving and ever-memorable service.

Jaffa seen after occupation by allied forces

Taken the day the Turks launched the attack to recapture the city

The German convent situated on the Mount of Olives

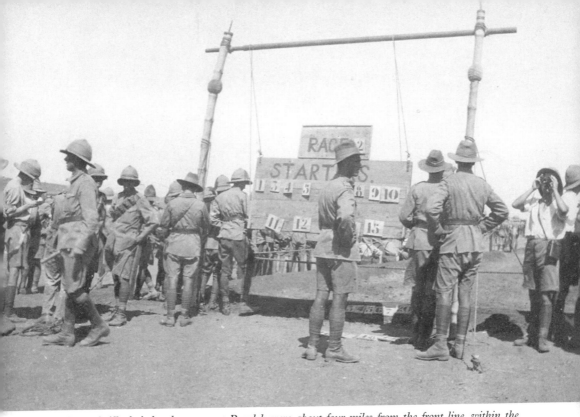

General Allenby's headquarters at Ramleh were about four miles from the front line, within the sound of the guns by day and in sight of their flashes by night. Tedium was broken by events we laid on such as the Ramleh Races

One night in April I was invited to dine with General Allenby. To my surprise he made me sit next to him. It was at the time when the last, big German offensive was being staged in France. He spoke to me very optimistically about the situation, although to the uninitiated like myself there seemed to be little cause as yet for any elation. General Allenby was not so tall as I expected him to be although his appearance was robust. He was not a great conversationalist but he gave the impression of having a limitless stock of common sense. He had a striking countenance with a determined jaw. General Clayton told me he had an ungovernable temper. But after all is said and done General Allenby was one of the greatest successes of the First World War.

One day I accompanied Clayton to a favourable position where we could watch the Turks in the effort to re-take Jerusalem. To get a better view I ascended to the top of the tower of the German convent situated on the Mount of Olives from where I had a wonderful panoramic view of the battle. A shell burst high up in the air uncomfortably close to the grandstand I had selected.

Self at Allenby's HQ

A day or two afterwards I went up, with another officer, to have a look at the Tabsor battlefield where there had been severe fighting. We wanted to note the effect of the new range-finding by sound. It was apparently perfect as we discovered all the enemy guns knocked out. The Turkish trenches presented a horrible spectacle. The hot sun of the last two days had produced a horrible effect on the innumerable corpses that littered the ground. They were swollen to double their normal size. Their hands and faces were ebony-black. I came across some half a dozen still in a sitting posture. They were sitting round the ashes of what had been a camp fire. It was obvious that they had been killed simultaneously by shrapnel. The sight they presented was appalling. The sun had distorted them into the most gruesome and grotesque figures; their black hands were like small balloons, their faces, swollen to amazing proportions, were twisted into the most terrible grimaces. By the end of October the war with Turkey was for all practical purposes at an end and from all the various fronts optimistic news began to arrive.

A Turkish trench

Damascus Gate, Jerusalem

On one occasion I was told to accompany an Arab officer – who had deserted to our side – to Damascus. We motored along the line of the Turkish retreat and stayed the first night at Haifa where I slept on the veranda of the hotel. The next day we went across the Plain of Esdraelon past Acre, Tyre and Saida where we lunched with the Arab Military Governor.

My car

Travelling along the road to Damascus

We arrived at Beirut in the evening. There I dined with Wyndham Deedes, who was acting as Military Governor. My Arab officer told me he had fought with the Turks in the Dardanelles and had been at Anzac. Comparing notes with him we discover that at one time we must have been in the trenches opposite one another. We stayed two nights at Beirut and on Friday, November 1st we journeyed through the Lebanon to Damascus. It was a lovely route reminding me somewhat of the Corniche Road in the French Riviera. I was very glad to reach Damascus without having broken down on the road as we were by ourselves unescorted. The country was infested with hostile Bedouins who would have thought nothing of doing away with us. While I was in Damascus I had the honour and privilege of having a personal interview with King Feisal the First. He was a most impressive figure, very tall and extremely handsome in his flowing robes. He had been a good friend to England on the whole, but the suggested settlement of the Middle East was not altogether to his liking. At the time of my interview with him the Allies would not allow him to have Damascus as his capital: 'You have taken from me my heart' I heard him murmur.

Dome of the Rock, Jerusalem

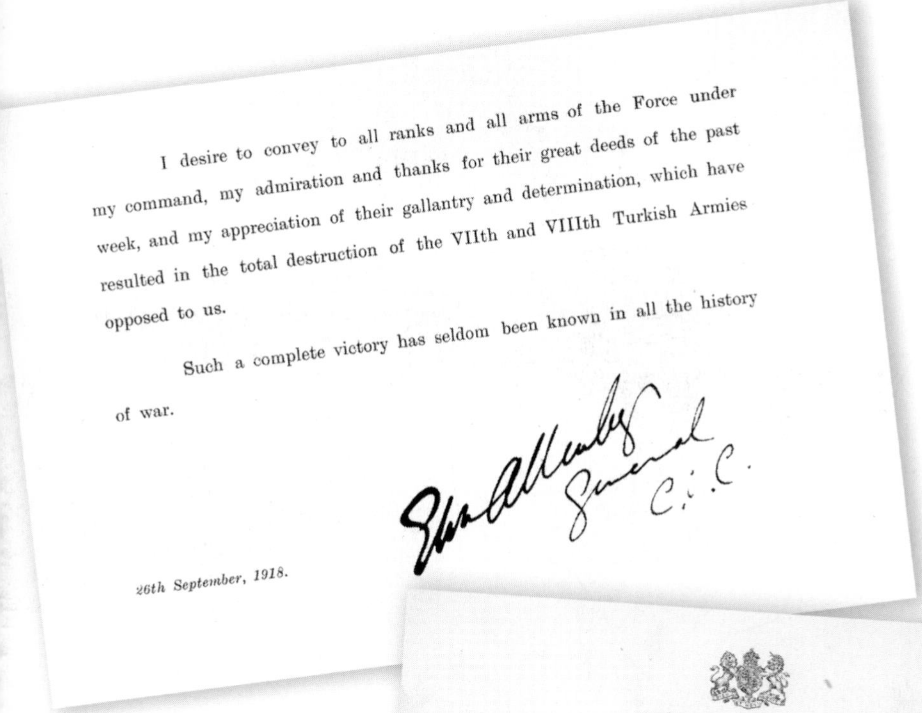

I desire to convey to all ranks and all arms of the Force under my command, my admiration and thanks for their great deeds of the past week, and my appreciation of their gallantry and determination, which have resulted in the total destruction of the VIIth and VIIIth Turkish Armies opposed to us.

Such a complete victory has seldom been known in all the history of war.

Edm Allenby
General
C in C.

26th September, 1918.

Notes of appreciation for services rendered from Churchill and Allenby

The War of 1914-1918.

Intelligence Corps

Capt. [T/Maj.] The Hon. E.C.G.Cadogan, Suff.Yeo.[T.F.]

was mentioned in a Despatch from

General Sir E.H.H. Allenby, G.C.B., G.C.M.G.

dated 5th March 1919.

for gallant and distinguished services in the Field.
I have it in command from the King to record His Majesty's
high appreciation of the services rendered.

War Office
Whitehall, S.W.
1st July 1919.

Winston S. Churchill
Secretary of State for War.

It was the morning of the 11th November and I rode out to inspect the ground where the Bucks Yeomanry had made a successful cavalry charge, one of the few that were recorded in the First World War. In the evening on my return, just as I was approaching GHQ, a staff officer met me and told me that the Germans had asked for an armistice. And so the war was at last ended. And how different the end of it was for me compared to what I so often imagined it would be. For myself it was a complete anticlimax. I felt deeply that I should have received the news in the trenches with my regiment.

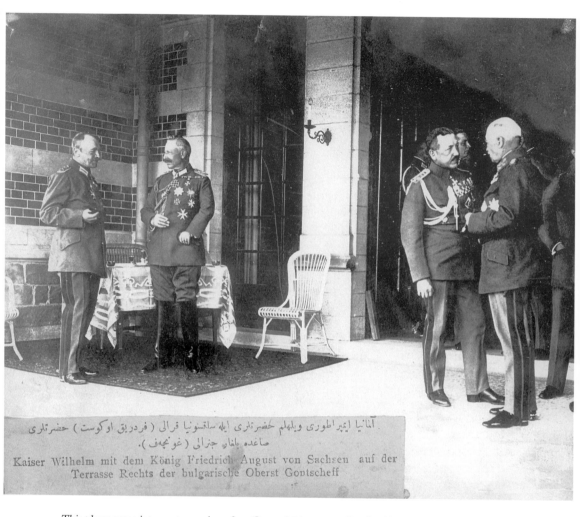

آلمانیا ایمپراطورى ویلهلم حضرتلرى ایله ساقسونیا قرالى (فردریق اوكوست) حضرتلرى
صاعده بلغار جنرالى (غونجهف).

Kaiser Wilhelm mit dem König Friedrich August von Sachsen auf der
Terrasse Rechts der bulgarische Oberst Goutscheff

*This photo came into my possession when General Limon von Sanders' Headquarters was captured
and his possessions ransacked*

Postscript

The weeks succeeding the armistice were tedious, made worse by the fact that owing to limited transport facilities and owing to the fact that officers were required to 'clear up', there seemed little chance of getting home for some time to come. That probably would have been the case for me had I not got my leg injured during the 'clear up' operations. It did not seem much at the time and since it was giving me little pain I continued with activities as best I could. It was little compared to the injuries of others. I set my mind to ignore it and got on with the job in hand. After a few days it was still swollen to twice its normal size and had become rather discoloured. One of my brother officers talked me into seeing the doctor who hurried me off to Ludd, the nearest casualty clearing station. I was placed in an overcrowded marquee tent along with a large number of sick and wounded – surgical and medical cases cheek by jowl. The boy in the bed next to me had a temperature of 105°. I expect it was cholera, smallpox or enteric; a dangerous bedfellow! I was operated on the next day in a tent. This was a memorable experience as the surgeon started on me before I was properly under the influence of the anaesthetic. I remember the feel of the knife penetrating my flesh though I was anaesthetised enough not to feel pain.

When I came to I was ordered to lay absolutely flat and quiet without moving for several weeks. I spent New Year's day, 1919 flat on my back at hospital in Belah.

The doctors decided that I should be sent home. Laid flat on my back all the way I was a 'stretcher case' from Ludd to London.

On Monday 20th January, 1919 I arrived at Southampton and was deposited in a train to Waterloo where I was met by a Red Cross official who informed me as to what military hospital I was allocated. The first evening in hospital friends and relatives came to see me, including the Speaker – Lord Ullswater. It was good to be alive amongst them once more.

Up to a point I had been content to remain in bed, free from care and responsibility, but it became irksome, this inactivity. I welcomed the day when I was allowed to hobble about on a crutch and renew my acquaintance with my ordinary London routine.

There were two changes I noticed when I began to wander about again. Everyone seemed to be bent on the business of amusement and entertainment, and small blame to anyone on that account. For four years everyone has been in a state of combined suspense, distress and anxiety. I remember so well hearing my sister rebuke her husband for some extravagance or other. He replied 'I don't care. I have had four rotten years and now I am going to enjoy myself.' That was the spirit of the time. The second phenomena that

D⁵A

(7 11 46) W150—RP4065 20,000 4/19 HWV(P124) H2824

WAR OFFICE,
LONDON,
S.W.1.

Any further communications on this subject should be addressed to—
The Secretary,
War Office,
London.
S.W.1,
and the following number quoted.

2 1 APR 1919

Ref/9/Suff.7co/648 M.S.4. (T.)

SIR,

I am commanded by the Army Council to inform you that in consequence of the demobilisation of the Army you have been disembodied as from the *21 — 3 — 19*

inclusive.

You will receive a further notification of any gratuity to which you may be entitled.

You should report any change of permanent address to the :—

Secretary (Ms 4ᵀ)
War Office London

I am also to take this opportunity of conveying the thanks of the Army Council for your services to the Country during the late war, and for the excellent work you have done.

I am,
SIR,
Your obedient Servant,

E.C.G. Cadogan
Lans Crescent Hotel.
Belgrave.
S.W.

R.H. Brade

My demobilization papers

21st February 1919.

Dear Sir,

I am desired by Mr. Cecil Beck to acknowledge your letter of the 20th instant, relative to the release of Capt. The Hon. Edward Cadogan.

Mr. Beck has put forward the case to the Demobilisation Department with a most urgent request that it may receive immediate attention.

Yours faithfully,

A. Hansen.

Private Secretary
to Parliamentary Secretary

F.C. Bramwell Esq.,
House of Commons.

impressed itself upon me was war-weariness. Everyone was tired of even talking about the war. It was only natural when both men and women – millions of them, had all had such unusual experiences at home and abroad that no-one was suffered to ask or talk about their experiences. By the same token there was little enough consideration by this time shown to the wounded. I remember well the sympathy they invoked in the first year of the war. But now they were hustled in tubes and buses just as much as any uninjured civilian would be.

London was full of the new type of officer, not yet demobilized and enjoying their fling to the utmost of their capacity. Here were young men, the majority of whom had probably not had as much as 'a fiver' to spend in their lives before, suddenly being presented with a gift in three figures. They were revelling in a life they had never been accustomed to before.

Finally what struck me most on my return to London were the crowds everywhere. I have never seen anything like it before or since. Every train was absolutely packed. There was a general restlessness through the country and everyone seemed to have money to burn.

On Friday, 21st March, 1919 I was demobilized. I was merely told to report at a certain address in Sloane Street. It was a very simple process, merely signing my name, which I could not help contrasting with my mobilization on 4th August, 1914.

I was proud to have been in uniform from the day the war broke out until it ended. For over three years I was a serving soldier with my regiment.

After I had completely recovered I resumed my old life as Secretary to the Speaker of the House of Commons.

Glossary

Apollo Belvederes	Able seamen
ASC	Army Service Corps
Bandolier	Shoulder belt for cartridges
Brocks	Heavy bombardment
Cap comforter	Cap that went down the neck and had flaps to go over the ears
Coaling	Re-stocking the ship with coal
Defile	Narrow gorge or pass through which troops can only march in single file
Dere	Deep stream-bed often modified and used as trenches
Dixies	Dixie can
Dubbing	Boot polish
EMB field hospital	Embarkation field hospital
Enteric	Typhoid fever
Fantasies	Water cans
Gazette	Military list
German taubes	Single-place single-engine monoplane used for observation and training
GOC	General officer commanding
Grenadier party	Sneaking over to enemy trenches and throwing in grenades
Hog a horse's mane	To cut the horse's mane so short that the hair sticks up like a hog's bristles
Housewife	Darning/sewing kit
Jaeger blanket	Blankets invented by Dr Jaeger specifically for outdoor use
Jheel	A shallow lake

Job's comforter	Woollen scarf
Lighter	Small craft used for landing supplies and men etc
Middies	Midshipmen
Mudir	Governor of an Egyptian province
MLO	Military landing officer
Narrows	The narrowest strip of water in the Dardanelles Straits
NCO	Non-commissioned officer
Nullah	Gully or stream-bed that remains dry except during the rainy season (see *wadi* – Arabic term)
OC	Officer commanding
Omda	Indian mayor
Over	When the shells go further than the intended target
Paliasse	Straw mattress
Parados	The other side of the trench from the parapet
Putties	Bandages that were wound around the leg from the top of the boot to the knee
RAMC	Royal Army Medical Corps
RE	Royal Engineer
Red hat	From the rank of colonel upwards a red band was worn around the hat
Sap	Stealth approach path
Spirits of wine	Alcohol used like methylated spirits
Stand to	To be prepared and ready for action
Strafe	Fierce attack
Talk lamp	Lamp used for signalling
Tommy's cooker	Small tin filled with paraffin jelly that you light and put your mess tin on top
Very pistol	Pistol that fired coloured flares
View Halloo	A hunting cry
Wadi	Gully or stream-bed that remains dry except during the rainy season (see *nullah* – Indian/Pakistani term)
White ducks	Naval officer's trousers